STEPPING HEAVENWARD

Selections from the Classic Story

by Elizabeth Prentiss

BARBOUR
PUBLISHING

© 2004 by Barbour Publishing, Inc.

Edited by Hope Clarke.

ISBN 1-59310-233-X

All Scripture quotations are from the King James Version of the Bible.

Cover image © PhotoDisc

Published by Barbour Publishing, Inc., P.O. Box 719, Uhrichsville, Ohio 44683, www.barbourbooks.com

Our mission is to publish and distribute inspirational products offering exceptional value and biblical encouragement to the masses.

ecpa Member of the
Evangelical Christian
Publishers Association

Printed in the United States of America.
5 4 3 2 1

INTRODUCTORY NOTE

Elizabeth Prentiss was born at Portland, Me., on October 26, 1818, and died, after a brief illness, at Dorset, Vt., on August 13, 1878. She was the youngest daughter of the Rev. Edward Payson, D.D., a very eminent servant of Christ, whose praise is still in all the churches.

At the age of sixteen, she began to write for the press: the little volume entitled *Only a Dandelion*, consisting chiefly of her early contributions to *The Youth's Companion* of Boston. The works by which she is best known are *Little Susy's Six Birthdays*, with its companions, and *Stepping Heavenward*. The latter was first published in 1869. It has passed through many editions in this country and has had a very wide circulation in Great Britain, Canada, and Australia. It was also translated into French and German, and several editions of it have been issued in those languages. It appeared at Leipsic in Tauchnitz's *Collection of British Authors*. Among Mrs. Prentiss's other works, which have been widely circulated both at home and abroad, are *The Flower of the Family, Little Lou's Sayings and Doings, Henry and Bessie, Fred and Maria and Me, The Percys, Nidworth and His Three Magic Wands, The Story Lizzie Told, The Home at Greylock, Aunt Jane's Hero, Urbane and His Friends, Pemaquid,* and *Golden Hours; or, Hymns and Songs of the Christian Life*.

The aim of her writings, whether designed for young or old, is to incite to patience, fidelity, hope, and all goodness by showing how trust in God and loving obedience to His blessed will brighten the darkest paths and make a heaven upon earth.

Of her religious character, the keynote is struck in her own hymn, "More Love to Thee, O Christ." That was her ruling passion in life and death. Writing to a young friend from Dorset, in 1873, she says: "To love Christ more—this is the deepest need, the constant cry of my soul. Down in the bowling alley, and out in the woods, and on my bed, and out driving, when I am happy and busy, and when I am sad and idle, the whisper keeps going up for more love, more love, more love!"

JANUARY 15, 1831—

How dreadfully old I am getting! Sixteen! Well, I don't see as I can help it. There it is in the big Bible in Father's own hand: "Katherine, born Jan. 15, 1815."

I meant to get up early this morning, but it looked dismally cold out-of-doors and felt delightfully warm in bed. So I covered myself up and made ever so many good resolutions.

I determined, in the first place, to begin this journal. To be sure, I have begun half a dozen and got tired of them after a while. Not tired of writing them, but disgusted with what I had to say of myself. But this time I mean to go on, in spite of everything. It will do me good to read it over and see what a creature I am.

Then I resolved to do more to please Mother than I have done.

And I determined to make one more effort to conquer my hasty temper. I thought, too, I would be self-denying this winter, like the people one reads about in books. I fancied how surprised and pleased everybody would be to see me so much improved!

Time passed quickly amid these agreeable thoughts, and I was quite startled to hear the bell ring for prayers. I jumped up in a great flurry and dressed as quickly as I could. Everything conspired together to plague me. I could not find a clean collar or a handkerchief. It is always just so. Mother is forever poking my things into out-of-the-way places! When at last I went down, they were all at breakfast.

"I hoped you would celebrate your birthday, dear, by coming down in good season," said Mother.

I do hate to be found fault with, so I fired up in an instant.

"If people hide my things so that I can't find them, of course I have to be late," I said. And I rather think I said it in a very cross way, for Mother sighed a little. I wish Mother wouldn't sigh. I would rather be called names out and out.

The moment breakfast was over, I had to hurry off to school. Just as I was going out, Mother said, "Have you your overshoes, dear?"

"Oh, Mother, don't slow me down! I shall be late," I said. "I don't need overshoes."

"It snowed all night and I think you do need them," Mother said.

"I don't know where they are. I hate overshoes. Do let me go, Mother," I cried. "I do wish I could ever have my own way."

"You shall have it now, my child," Mother said and went away.

Now what was the use of her calling me "my child" in such a tone, I should like to know.

I hurried off, and just as I got to the door of the schoolroom, it flashed into my mind that I had not said my prayers! A nice way to begin on one's birthday to be sure! Well, I had no time. And perhaps my good resolutions pleased God almost as much as one of my rambling, stupid prayers could. For I must admit I can't make good prayers. I can't think of anything to say. I often wonder what Mother finds to say when she is shut up by the hour praying.

I had a pretty good time at school. My teachers

praised me, and Amelia seemed so fond of me! She brought me a birthday present, a purse that she had knit for me herself and a net for my hair. Nets are just coming into fashion. It will save a good deal of time my having this one. Instead of combing and combing and combing my hair to get it glossy enough to suit Mother, I can just give it one twist and one squeeze, and the whole thing will be settled for the day.

Amelia wrote me a dear little note with her presents. I do really believe she loves me dearly. It is so nice to have people love you!

When I got home, Mother called me into her room. She looked as if she had been crying. She said I gave her a great deal of pain by my self-will and ill temper and conceit.

"Conceit!" I screamed out. "Oh, Mother, if you only knew how horrid I think I am!"

Mother smiled a little. Then she went on with her list till she made me out the worst creature in the world. I burst out crying and was running off to my room, but she made me come back and hear the rest. She said my character would be essentially formed by the time I reached my twentieth year and left it to me to decide if I wished to be as a woman what I was now as a girl. I felt sulky and would not answer. I was shocked to think I had got only four years in which to improve, but, after all, a good deal could be done in that time. Of course I don't want to be always exactly what I am now.

Mother went on to say that I had in me the elements of a fine character if I would only conquer some of my faults. "You are frank and truthful," she said, "and in some things conscientious. I hope you are really a child of God and are trying to please Him. And it is my daily prayer that you may become a lovely, loving, useful woman."

I made no answer. I wanted to say something, but

my tongue wouldn't move. I was angry with Mother and angry with myself. At last everything came out all in a rush, mixed up with such floods of tears that I thought Mother's heart would melt and that she would take back what she had said.

"Amelia's mother never talks so to her!" I said. "She praises her and tells her what a comfort she is to her. But just as I am trying as hard as I can to be good, and making resolutions and all that, you scold me and discourage me!"

Mother's voice was very soft and gentle as she asked, "Do you call this 'scolding,' my child?"

"And I don't like to be called conceited," I went on. "I know I am perfectly horrid, and I am just as unhappy as I can be."

"I am very sorry for you, dear," Mother replied. "But you must bear with me. Other people will see your faults, but only your mother will have the courage to speak of them. Now go to your room, and wipe away the traces of your tears so the rest of the family won't know that you have been crying on your birthday." She kissed me, but I did not kiss her. I really believe Satan himself hindered me. I ran across the hall to my room, slammed the door, and locked myself in. I was going to throw myself on the bed and cry till I was sick. Then I should look pale and tired, and they would all pity me. I do like so to be pitied! But on the table, by the window, I saw a beautiful new desk in place of the old clumsy thing I had been spattering and spoiling so many years. A little note, full of love, said it was from Mother and begged me every day of my life to read and reflect upon a few verses of a tastefully bound copy of the Bible that accompanied the desk. "A few verses," she said, "carefully read and pondered, instead of a chapter or two read for mere form's sake." I looked at my desk, which contained exactly what I wanted, plenty of paper, seals, wax, and pens. I always use wax. Wafers are vulgar. Then I opened the Bible at random and lighted on these words: "Watch therefore: for ye know not what hour your Lord doth come" (Matt. 24:42). There was nothing very cheering in that. I felt a real repugnance to be always on the watch, thinking I might die at any moment. I am sure I am not fit to die. Besides, I want to have a good time with nothing to worry me. I hope I shall live ever so long. Perhaps in the course of forty or fifty years I may get tired of this world and want to leave it. And I hope by that time I shall be a great deal better than I am now and fit to go to heaven.

I wrote a note to Mother on my new desk and thanked her for it. I told her she was the best mother in the world and that I was the worst daughter. When it was done, I did not like it, and so I wrote another. Then I went down to dinner and felt better. We had such a nice dinner! Everything I liked best was on the table. Mother had not forgotten one of all the dishes I like. Amelia was there, too. Mother had invited her to give me a little surprise. It is bedtime now, and I must say my prayers and go to bed. I have got all chilled through, writing here in the cold. I believe I will say my prayers in bed, just for this once. I do not feel sleepy, but I am sure I ought not to sit up another moment.

Feb. 20—

It has been quite a mild day for the season, and the doctor said I might drive out. I enjoyed getting the air very much. I feel just as well as ever and long to get back to school. I think God has been very good to me in making me well again, and I wish I loved Him better. But, oh, I am not sure I do love Him! I hate to own it to myself and to write it down here, but I will. I do not love to pray. I am always eager to get it over with and out of the way so as to have leisure to enjoy myself. I mean that this is usually so. This morning I cried a good deal while I was on my knees and felt sorry for my quick temper and all my bad ways. If I always felt so, perhaps praying would not be such a task. I wish I knew whether anybody exactly as bad as I am ever got to heaven at last? I have read ever so many memoirs, and they were all about people who were too good to live, and so died, or else went on a mission; I am not at all like any of them.

APRIL 2—

There are three of Mother's friends living near us, each with lots of little children. It is perfectly ridiculous how much those creatures are sick. They send for Mother if so much as a pimple comes out on one of their faces. When I have children, I don't mean to have such goings-on. I shall be careful about what they eat and keep them from getting cold, and they will keep well of their own accord. Mrs. Jones has just sent for Mother to see her Tommy. It was so provoking. I had coaxed Mother into letting me have a black silk apron; they are all the fashion now, embroidered in floss silk. I had drawn a lovely vine for mine entirely out of my own hand, and Mother was going to arrange the pattern for me when that message came and she had to go. I don't believe anything ails the child! A great chubby thing!

APRIL 3—

Poor Mrs. Jones! Her dear little Tommy is dead! I stayed at home from school today and had all the other children here to get them out of their mother's way. How dreadfully she must feel! Mother cried when she told me how the dear little fellow suffered in his last moments. It reminded her of my little brothers who died in the same way just before I was born. Dear Mother! I wonder how I can ever forget what troubles she has had, and am not always sweet and loving. She has gone now, where she always goes when she feels sad, straight to God. Of course she did not say so, but I know Mother.

JUNE 1—

Last Sunday Dr. Cabot preached to the young. He first addressed those who knew they did not love God. It did not seem to me that I belonged to that class. Then he spoke to those who knew they did. I felt sure I was not one of those. Last of all he spoke affectionately to those who did not know what to think, and I was frightened and ashamed to feel tears running down my cheeks when he said that he believed that most of his hearers who were in this doubtful state did really love their Master, only their love was something as new and as tender and perhaps as unobserved as the tiny point of green that, forcing its way through the earth, is yet unconscious of its own existence but promises a thrifty plant. I don't suppose I express it very well, but I know what he meant. He then invited those belonging to each class to meet him on three successive Saturday afternoons. I shall certainly go.

JULY 27—

I was rushing through the hall just after I wrote that [I was going to Amelia's] and met Mother.

"I am going to Amelia's," I said, hurrying past her.

"Stop one minute, dear. Dr. Cabot is downstairs. He says he has been expecting a visit from you, but as you did not come to him, he has come to you."

"I wish he would mind his own business," I said.

"I think he is minding it, dear," Mother answered. "His Master's business is his, and that has brought him here. Go to him, my darling child; I am sure you crave something better than prizes and compliments and new dresses and journeys."

If anybody but Mother had said that, my heart would have melted at once, and I should have gone right down to Dr. Cabot to be molded in his hands to almost any shape. But as it was, I brushed past her, ran into my room, and locked my door. Oh, what makes me act so! I hate myself for it; I don't want to do it!

Last week I dined with Mrs. Jones. Her little Tommy that died was very fond of me, and that, I suppose, makes her have me there so often. Lucy was at the table and very fractious. She cried first for one thing and then for another. At last her mother in a gentle, but very decided way, put her down from the table. Then she cried louder than ever. But when her mother offered to take her back if she would be good, she screamed yet more. She wanted to come and wouldn't let herself come. I almost hated her when I saw her act so, and now I am behaving ten times worse, and I am just as miserable as I can be.

JULY 29—

Amelia has been here. She has had another talk with Dr. Cabot and is perfectly happy. She says it is so easy to be a Christian! It may be easy for her; everything is. She never has any of my dreadful feelings and does not understand them when I try to explain them to her. Well! If I am fated to be miserable, I must try to bear it.

Oct. 23—

I am so glad that my studies are harder this year, as I am never happy except when every moment is occupied. However, I do not study all the time, by any means. Amelia's mother, Mrs. Gordon, grows more and more fond of me and has me there to dinner or to tea continually. She has a much higher opinion of me than Mother has and is always saying the sort of things that make you feel nice. She holds me up to Amelia as an example, begging her to imitate me in my fidelity about my lessons and declaring there is nothing she so much desires as to have a daughter as bright and original like me. Amelia only laughs and goes and purrs in her mother's ears when she hears such talk. It costs her nothing to be pleasant. She was born so. For my part, I think myself lucky to have such a friend. She gets along with my odd, hateful ways better than anyone else does.

Mother, when I boast of this, says Amelia has no penetration into character and that she would be fond of almost anyone fond of her and that the fury with which I love her deserves some response. I really don't know what to make of Mother. Most people are proud of their children when they see others admire them; but she does say such poky things! Of course I know that having a gift for music and a taste for drawing and a reputation for saying witty, bright things isn't enough. But when she doesn't find fault with me and nothing happens to keep me down, I am the gayest creature on earth. I do love to get with a lot of nice girls and carry on! I have got enough fun in me to keep a houseful merry. And Mother needn't say anything. I inherited it from her.

EVENING—

I knew it was coming! Mother has been in to see what I was about and to give me a bit of her mind. She says she loves to see me gay and cheerful, as is natural at my age, but that so much levity quite upsets and disorders the mind, indisposing it for serious thoughts.

"But, Mother," I said, "didn't you carry on when you were a young girl?"

"Of course I did," she said, smiling. "But I do not think I was quite so thoughtless as you are."

"Thoughtless" indeed! I wish I were! But am I not always full of uneasy, reproachful thoughts when the moment of excitement is over? Other girls, who seem less trifling than I, are really more so. Their heads are full of dresses and parties and beaux and all that sort of nonsense. I wonder if that ever worries their mothers, or whether mine is the only one who weeps in secret? Well, I shall be young but once, and while I am, do let me have a good time!

SUNDAY, NOV. 20—

Oh, the difference between this day and the day I wrote that! There are no good times in this dreadful world. I have hardly courage or strength to write down the history of the past few weeks. The day after I had deliberately made up my mind to enjoy myself, cost what it might, my dear father called me to him, kissed me, pulled my ears a little, and gave me some money.

"We have had to keep you rather low on funds," he said, laughing. "But I recovered this amount yesterday, and as it was a little debt I had given up, I can spare it to you. Girls like pin money, I know, and you may spend this just as you please."

I was delighted. I want to take more drawing lessons but did not feel sure he could afford it. Besides—I am a little ashamed to write it down—I knew somebody had been praising me, or Father would not have seemed so fond of me. I wondered who it was and felt a good deal puffed up. "After all," I said to myself, "some people like me even if I have got my faults." I threw my arms around his neck and kissed him, though that cost me a great effort. I never like to show what I feel. But, oh! how thankful I am for it now.

As to Mother, I know Father never goes without kissing her good-bye.

I went out with her to take a walk at three o'clock. We had just reached the corner of Orange Street when I saw a carriage driving slowly toward us; it appeared to be full of sailors. Then I saw our friend, Mr. Freeman, among them. When he saw us, he jumped out and came up to us. I do not know what he said. I saw Mother turn pale and catch at his arm as if she were afraid of falling. But she did not speak a word.

"Oh! Mr. Freeman, what is it?" I cried out. "Has anything happened to Father? Is he hurt? Where is he?"

"He is in the carriage," he said. "We are taking him home. He has had a fall."

Then we went on in silence. The sailors were carrying Father in as we reached the house. They laid him on the sofa, and we saw his poor head—

NOV. 23—

I will try to write the rest now. Father was alive but insensible. He had fallen down into the hold of the ship, and the sailors heard him groaning there. He lived three hours after they brought him home. Mr. Freeman and all our friends were very kind. But we like best to be alone, we three, Mother and James and I. Poor Mother looks twenty years older, but she is so patient and so concerned for us and has such a smile of welcome for everyone that comes in that it breaks my heart to see her.

NOV. 28—

I believe I shall go crazy unless people stop coming here, hurling volleys of texts at Mother and me. When soldiers drop wounded on the battlefield, they are taken up tenderly and carried "to the rear," which means, I suppose, out of sight and sound. Is anybody mad enough to suppose it will do them any good to hear Scripture quoted—sermons launched at them before their open, bleeding wounds are staunched?

Mother assents, in a mild way, when I talk so and says, "Yes, yes, we are indeed lying wounded on the battlefield of life and in no condition to listen to any words save those of pity. But, dear Katy, we must interpret aright all the well-meant attempts of our friends to comfort us. They mean sympathy, however awkwardly they express it."

JAN. 1, 1832—

People talk a great deal about the blessed effects of sorrow. But I do not see any good it has done me to lose my dear father, and as for Mother, she was good enough before.

We are going to leave our pleasant home, where all of us children were born, and move into a house in an out-of-the-way street. By selling this house and renting a smaller one, Mother hopes, with economy, to carry James through college. And I must go to Miss Higgins's school because it is less expensive than Mr. Stone's. Miss Higgins, indeed! I never could bear her! A few months ago, how I should have cried and stormed at the idea of her school. But the great sorrow swallows up the little trial.

I tried once more, this morning, as it is the first day of the year, to force myself to begin to love God.

I want to do it; I know I ought to do it; but I cannot. Every day now I go through the form of saying something that I try to pass off as praying. But I take no pleasure in it, as good people say they do and as I am sure Mother does. Nobody could live in the house with her and doubt that.

SUNDAY, AUG. 5—

Jenny's brother has been at our church all day. He walked home with me this afternoon. Mother, after being up all night with Mrs. Jones and her baby, was not able to go out.

Dr. Cabot preaches as if we had all got to die pretty soon or else have something almost as bad happen to us. How can old people always try to make young people feel uncomfortable and as if things couldn't last?

AUG. 25—

Jenny says her brother is perfectly fascinated with me and that I must try to like him in return. I suppose Mother would say my head was turned by my good fortune, but it is not. I am getting quite sober and serious. It is a great thing to be—to be—well. . .liked. I have seen some verses of his composition today that show that he is all heart and soul and would make any sacrifice for one he loved. I could not like a man who did not possess such sentiments as his.

Perhaps Mother would think I ought not to put such things into my journal.

Jenny has thought of such a splendid plan! What a dear little thing she is! She and her brother are so much alike!

The plan is for us three girls—Jenny, Amelia, and myself—to form ourselves into a little class to read and to study together. She says "Charley" will direct our readings and help us with our studies. It is perfectly delightful.

SEPTEMBER 1—

Somehow I forgot to tell Mother that Mr. Underhill was to be our teacher. So when it came my turn to have the class meet here, she was not quite pleased. I told her she could stay in the room and watch us, and then she would see for herself that we all behaved ourselves.

SEPT. 28—

We met at Jenny's this evening. Amelia had a bad head-ache and could not come. Jenny idled over her lessons and at last took a book and began to read. I studied awhile with Mr. Underhill. At last he said, scribbling something on a bit of paper, "Here is a sentence I hope you can translate."

I took it and read these words:

"You are the brightest, prettiest, most warmhearted little thing in the world. And I love you more than tongue can tell. You must love me in the same way."

I felt hot and then cold and then glad and then sorry. But I pretended to laugh and said I could not translate Greek. I shall have to tell Mother, and what will she say!

Oct. 1—

I never can write down all the things that have happened. The very day after I wrote Jenny that Mother had forbidden my going to the class, Charley came to see Mother, and they had a regular fight together. He has told me about it since. Then, as he could not prevail, his uncle wrote, told her it would be the making of Charley to be settled down on one young lady instead of hovering from flower to flower, as he was doing now. Then Jenny came with her pretty ways and cried and told Mother what a darling brother Charley was. She made a good deal, too, out of his having lost both father and mother and needing my affection so much. Mother shut herself up and, I have no doubt, prayed over it. I really believe she prays over every new dress she buys. Then she sent for me and talked beautifully, and I behaved abominably.

At last she said she would put us on one year's probation. Charley might spend one evening here every two weeks, when she should always be present. We were never to be seen together in public, nor would she allow us to correspond. If, at the end of the year, we were both as eager for it as we are now, she would consent to our engagement. Of course we shall be, so I consider myself as good as engaged now. Dear me! How funny it seems.

Oct. 1, 1833—

The year of probation is over, and I have nothing to do now but to be happy. But being engaged is not half so nice as I expected it would be. I suppose it is owing to my being obliged to defy Mother's judgment in order to gratify my own. People say she has great insight into character and sees, at a glance, what others only learn after much study.

Nov. 1—

I really think I am sick and going to die. Last night I raised a little blood. I dare not tell Mother; it would distress her so; but I am sure it came from my lungs. Charley said last week he really must stay away till I got better, for my cough sounded like his mother's. I have been very lonely and have shed some tears, but most of the time have been too sorrowful to cry. If we were married and I had a cough, would he go and leave me, I wonder?

Jan. 26, 1834—

I have shut myself up in my room today to think over things. The end of it is that I am full of mortification and confusion of face. If I had only had confidence in Mother's judgment I should never have got entangled in this silly engagement. I see now that Charley never could have made me happy, and I know there is a good deal in my heart he never called out. I wish, however, I had not written him when I was in such a passion. No wonder he is thankful that he has got free from such a vixen. But, oh!

the provocation was terrible!

I have made up my mind never to tell a human soul about this affair. It will be so high-minded and honorable to shield him thus from the contempt he deserves. With all my faults I am glad that there is nothing mean or little about me!

FEB. 4—

The name of Charley Underhill appears on these pages for the last time. He is engaged to Amelia! From this moment she is lost to me forever. How desolate, how mortified, how miserable I am! Who could have thought this of Amelia? She came to see me, radiant with joy. I concealed my disgust until she said that Charley felt now that he had never really loved me but had preferred her all along. Then I burst out. What I said I do not know and do not care. The whole thing is so disgraceful that I should be a stock or a stone not to resent it.

FEB. 6—

Now that it is all over, how ashamed I am of the fury I have been in and which has given Amelia such advantage over me! I was beginning to believe that I was really living a feeble and fluttering but real Christian life and finding some satisfaction in it. But that is all over now. I am doomed to be a victim of my own unstable, passionate, wayward nature; and the sooner I settle down into that conviction, the better. And yet how my very soul craves the highest happiness and refuses to be comforted while that is wanting.

FEB. 7—

After writing that, I do not know what made me go to see Dr. Cabot. He received me in that cheerful way of his that seems to promise he will take one's burden right off one's back.

"I am very glad to see you, my dear child," he said.

I intended to be very dignified and cold. As if I was going to have any Dr. Cabots undertaking to sympathize with me! But those few kind words just upset me, and I began to cry.

"You would not speak so kindly," I got out at last, "if you knew what a dreadful creature I am. I am angry with myself and angry with everybody and angry with God. I can't be good two minutes at a time. I do everything I do not want to do and do nothing I try and pray to do. Everybody plagues me and tempts me. And God does not answer any of my prayers, and I am just desperate."

"Poor child!" he said in a low voice, as if to himself. "Poor, heartsick, tired child that cannot see what I can see, that its Father's loving arms are all about it!"

I stopped crying to strain my ears to listen. He went on.

"Katy, all that you say may be true. I daresay it is. But God loves you. He loves you."

He loves me, I repeated to myself. *He loves me*. "Oh, Dr. Cabot, if I could believe that! If I could believe that, after all the promises I have broken, all the foolish, wrong things I have done and shall always be doing, God perhaps still loves me!"

"You may be sure of it," he said solemnly. "I, His minister, bring the gospel to you today. Go home and say over and over to yourself, 'I am a wayward, foolish child. But He loves me! I have disobeyed and grieved Him ten thousand times. But He loves me! I have lost faith in some of my dearest friends and am very desolate. But He loves me! I do not love Him; I am even angry with Him! But He loves me!' "

I came away; and all the way home I fought this battle with myself, saying, "He loves me!" I knelt down to pray, and all my wasted, childish, wicked life came and stared me in the face. I looked at it and said with tears of joy, "But He loves me!" Never in my life did I feel so rested, so quieted, so sorrowful, and yet so satisfied.

MARCH 25—

Mother is very much astonished to see how nicely I am keeping things in order. I was flying about this morning, singing and dusting the furniture, when she came in and began, "He that is faithful in that which is least"—but I ran at her with my brush and would not let her finish. I really, really don't deserve to be praised. For I have been thinking that, if it is true that God notices every little thing we do to please Him, He must also notice every cross word we speak, every shrug of the shoulders, every ungracious look, and that they displease Him. And my list of such offenses is as long as my life!

APRIL 6—

I have taken it at last. I would not take one before, because I knew I could not teach little children how to love God unless I loved Him myself. My class is perfectly delightful. There are twelve dear little things in it of all ages between eight and nine. Eleven are girls, and the one boy makes me more trouble than all of them put together. When I get them all about me and their sweet innocent faces look up into mine, I am so happy that I can hardly help stopping every now and then to kiss them. They ask the very strangest questions! I mean to spend a great deal of time in preparing the lesson and in hunting up stories to illustrate it. Oh, I am so glad I was ever born into this beautiful world, where there will always be dear little children to love!

JULY 29—

It is high time to stop and think. I have been like one running a race and am stopping to take breath. I do not like the way in which things have been going on of late. I feel restless and ill at ease. I see that if I would be happy in God, I must give Him all. And there is a wicked reluctance to do that. I want Him—but I want to have my own way, too. I want to walk humbly and softly before Him, and I want to go where I shall be admired and applauded. To whom shall I yield? To God? Or to myself?

JANUARY 24, 1835—

A message came yesterday morning from Susan Green to the effect that she had had a dreadful fall and was half-killed. Mother wanted to set off at once to see her, but I would not let her go, as she has one of her worst colds. She then asked me to go in her place. I turned up my nose at the bare thought, though I daresay it turns up enough on its own account.

"Oh, Mother!" I said, reproachfully, "That dirty old woman!"

Mother made no answer, and I sat down at the piano and played a little. But I only played discords.

"Do you think it is my duty to run after such horrid old women?" I asked Mother at last.

"I think, dear, you must make your own duties," she said kindly. "I daresay that at your age I should have made a great deal out of my personal repugnance to such a woman as Susan and very little out of her sufferings."

I believe I am the most fastidious creature in the world. Sickrooms, with their intolerable smells of camphor and vinegar and mustard, their gloom and their whines and their groans, actually make me shudder. But was it now just such fastidiousness that made Cha—no, I won't utter his name—that made somebody weary of my possibilities? And has that terrible lesson really done me no good?

JAN. 27—

I have learned one thing, by yesterday's experience [Susan's death], that is worth knowing. It is this: Duty looks more repelling at a distance than when fairly faced and met. Of course I have read the lines,

> Nor know we anything so fair
> As is the smile upon thy face;

but I seem to be one of the stupid sort who never apprehend a thing till they experience it. Now, however, I have seen the smile and find it so "fair" that I shall gladly plod through many a hardship and trial to meet it again.

Poor Susan! Perhaps God heard my eager prayer for her soul and revealed Himself to her at the very last moment.

MARCH 2—

Such a strange thing has happened! Susan Green left a will bequeathing her precious savings to whoever offered the last prayer in her hearing! I do not want, I never could touch a penny of that hardly earned store; and if I did want it, no earthly motive would tempt me to tell a human being that that last prayer was offered by me, an inexperienced, trembling girl, driven to it by mere desperation! So it has gone to Dr. Cabot, who will not use it for himself, I am sure, but will be delighted to have it to give to poor people, who really besiege him. The last time he called to see Susan, he talked and prayed with her and says she seemed pleased and grateful and promised to be more regular at church, which she had been ever since.

MARCH 31—

The more I pray and the more I read the Bible, the more I feel my ignorance. And the more earnestly I desire holiness, the more utterly unholy I see myself to be. But I have pledged myself to the Lord, and I must pay my vows, cost what it may.

I have begun to read Taylor's *Holy Living and Dying*. A month ago I should have found it a tedious, dry book. But I am reading it with a sort of avidity, like one seeking after hid treasure. Mother, observing what I was doing, advised me not to read it straight through but to mingle a passage now and then with chapters from other books. She suggested my beginning on Baxter's *Saints' Rest*, and of that I have read every word. I shall read it over, as Dr. Cabot advised, till I have fully caught its spirit. Even this one reading has taken away my lingering fear of death and made heaven wonderfully attractive. I never mean to read worldly books again, and my music and drawing I have given up forever.

NEW YORK, APRIL 16—

After all, Mother has come off conqueror, and here I am at Aunty's. After our quiet, plain little home in our quiet little town, this seems like a new world. The house is large, but it is as full as it can hold. Aunty has six children of her own and had adopted two. She says she always meant to imitate the old woman who lived in a shoe. She reminds me of Mother, and yet she is very different: full of fun and energy; flying about the house as on wings, with a kind, bright word for everybody. All her household affairs go on like clockwork; the children are always nicely dressed; nobody ever seems out of humor; nobody is ever sick. Aunty is the central object round which everybody revolves; you can't forget her a moment, for she is always doing something for you, and then her unflagging good humor and cheerfulness keep you good-humored and cheerful. I don't wonder Uncle Alfred loves her so!

I hope I shall have just such a home. I mean this is the sort of home I should like if I were married, which I never mean to be. I should like to be just such a bright, loving wife as Aunty is; to have my husband lean on me as Uncle leans on her; to have just as many children and to train them as wisely and kindly as she does hers. Then, indeed, I should feel that I had not been born in vain but had a high and sacred mission on earth. But as it is, I must just pick up what scraps of usefulness I can and let the rest go.

APRIL 30—

Aunty's baby, my dear father's namesake and hitherto the merriest little fellow I ever saw, was taken sick last night very suddenly. She sent for the doctor at once, who would not say positively what was the matter but this morning pronounced it scarlet fever. The three youngest have all come down with it today. If they were my children, I should be in a perfect worry and flurry. Indeed, I am as it is. But Aunty is as bright and cheerful as ever. She flies from one to another and keeps up their spirits with her own gaiety. I am mortified to find that at such a time as this I can think of myself and that I find it irksome to be shut up in sickrooms instead of walking, driving, visiting, and the like. But, as Dr. Cabot says, I can now choose to imitate my Master, who spent His whole life in doing good; and I do hope, too, to be of some little use to Aunty after her kindness to me.

MAY 15—

I was in a burning fever all night, and my head ached, and my throat was and is very sore. If I knew I was going to die, I would burn up this journal first. I would not have anyone see it for the world.

JUNE 1—

We are all as well as ever, but the doctor keeps some of the children still confined to the house for fear of bad consequences following the fever. He visits them twice a day for the same reason, or at least under that pretense, but I really believe he comes because he has got the habit of coming and because he admires Aunty so much. She has a real affection for him and is continually asking me if I don't like this and that quality in him, which I can't see at all. We begin to drive out again. The weather is very warm, but I feel perfectly well.

JULY 5—

Here I am again, safely at home, and very pleasant it seems to be with dear Mother again. I have told her about Dr. E. She says very little about it one way or the other.

JULY 10—

Mother sees that I am restless and out of sorts. "What is it, dear?" she asked this morning. "Has Dr. Elliott anything to do with the unsettled state you are in?"

"Why, no, Mother," I answered. "My going away has broken up all my habits; that's all. Still, if I knew Dr. Elliott did not care much and was beginning to forget it, I daresay I should feel better."

"If you were perfectly sure that you never could return his affection," she said, "you were quite right in telling him so at once. But if you had any misgivings on the subject, it would have been better to wait and to ask God to direct you."

Yes, it would. But at the moment, I had no misgivings. In my usual headlong style I settled one of the most weighty questions of my life without reflection, without so much as one silent appeal to God to tell me how to act. And now I have forever repelled and thrown away a heart that truly loved me. He will go his way and I shall go mine. He never will know what I am only just beginning to know myself, that I yearn after his love with unutterable yearning.

But I am not going to sit down in sentimental despondency to weep over this irreparable past. No human being could forgive such folly as mine; but God can. In my sorrowfulness and loneliness I fly to Him and find what is better than earthly felicity, the sweetest peace. He allowed me to bring upon myself, in one hasty moment, a shadow out of which I shall not soon pass; but He pities and He forgives me, and I have had many precious moments when I could say sincerely and joyfully, "Whom have I in heaven but thee? and there is none upon earth that I desire beside thee" (Ps. 73:25).

With a character still so undisciplined as mine, I seriously doubt whether I could have made him happy who has honored me with his unmerited affection. Sometimes I think I am as impetuous and as quick-tempered as ever; I get angry with dear Mother and with James, even, if they oppose me; how unfit, then, I am to become the mistress of a household and the wife of a good man!

How came he to love me? I cannot, cannot imagine!

AUGUST 31—

The last day of the very happiest summer I ever spent. If I had only been willing to believe the testimony of others, I might have been just as happy long ago. But I wanted to have all there was in God and all there was in the world at once; and there was a constant, painful struggle between the two. I hope that struggle is now over. I deliberately choose and prefer God. I have found a sweet peace in trying to please Him such as I never conceived of. I would not change it for all the best things this world can give.

But I have a great deal to learn. I am like a child who cannot run to get what he wants but approaches it step by step, slowly, timidly—and yet approaches it. I am amazed at the patience of my blessed Master and Teacher, but how I love His school!

SEPTEMBER—

This, too, has been a delightful month in a certain sense. Amelia's marriage, at which I had to be present, upset me a little, but it was but a little ruffle on a deep sea of peace.

I saw Dr. Cabot today. He is quite well again and speaks of Dr. Elliott's skill with rapture. He asked about my Sunday scholars and my poor folks, etc., and I could not help letting out a little of the joy that has taken possession of me.

"This is as it should be," he said. "I should be sorry to see a person of your temperament enthusiastic in everything save religion. Do not be discouraged if you still have some ups and downs. 'He that is down need fear no fall'; but you are away up on the heights and may have a fall now and then."

This made me a little uncomfortable. I don't want any falls. I want to go on to perfection.

OCT. 10—

We have very sad news from Aunty. She says my uncle is quite broken down with some obscure disease that has been creeping stealthily along for months. All his physicians agree that he must give up his business and try the effect of a year's rest. Dr. Elliott proposes his going to Europe, which seems to me about as formidable as going to the next world. Aunty makes the best she can of it, but she says the thought of being separated from Uncle a whole year is dreadful. I pray for her day and night that this wild project may be given up. Why, he would be on the ocean ever so many weeks, exposed to all the discomforts of narrow quarters and poor food, and that just as winter is drawing nigh!

OCT. 12—

Aunty writes that the voyage to Europe has been decided on and that Dr. Elliott is to accompany Uncle, travel with him, amuse him, and bring him home a well man. I hope Dr. E.'s power to amuse may exist somewhere, but I must own it was in a most latent form when I had the pleasure of knowing him. Poor Aunty! How much better it would be for her to go with Uncle! There are all the children, to be sure. Well, I hope Uncle may be the better for this great undertaking, but I don't like the idea of it.

OCT. 15—

Another letter from Aunty and new plans! The Dr. is to stay at home; Aunty is to go with Uncle, and we— Mother and myself—are to take possession of the house and the children during their absence! In other words, all this is to be if we say amen. Could anything be more frightful? To refuse would be selfish and cruel. If we consent, I thrust myself under Dr. Elliott's very nose.

OCT. 16—

Mother is surprised that I can hesitate one instant. She seems to have forgotten all about Dr. E. She says we can easily find a family to take this house for a year and that she is delighted to do anything for Aunty that can be done.

NOV. 4—

Here we are, the whole thing settled. Uncle and Aunty started a week ago, and we are monarchs of all we survey, and this is a great deal. I am determined that Mother shall not be worn-out with these children, although, of course, I could not manage them without her advice and help. It is to be hoped they won't all have the measles in a body or anything of that sort; I am sure it would be annoying to Dr. E. to come here now.

NOV. 25—

Of course the baby must go on teething if only to have the doctor sent for to lance his gums. I told Mother I was sure I could not be present when this was being done, so, though she looked surprised and said people should accustom themselves to such things, she volunteered to hold the baby herself.

DEC. 4—

Dr. Elliott came this morning to ask Mother to go with him to see a child who had met with a horrible accident.

She turned pale and pressed her lips together but went at once to get ready. Then my long-suppressed wrath burst out.

"How can you ask poor Mother to go and see such sights?" I cried. "You must think her nothing but a stone if you suppose that after the way in which my father died—"

"It was indeed most thoughtless of me," he interrupted. "But your mother is such a rare woman, so decided and self-controlled, yet so gentle, so full of tender sympathy, that I hardly know where else to look for just the help I need today. If you could see this poor child, even you would justify me."

"Even *you!*" you monster of selfishness, heart of stone, floating bubble, "even *you* would justify it!"

How cruel, how unjust, how unforgiving he is!

I rushed out of the room and cried until I was tired.

DEC. 6—

Mother says she feels really grateful to Dr. E. for taking her to see that child and to help soothe and comfort it while he went through with a severe, painful operation that she would not describe because she fancied I looked pale. I said I should think the child's mother the most proper person to soothe it on such an occasion.

"The poor thing has no mother," she said reproachfully. "What has got into you, Kate? You do not seem at all like yourself."

"I should think you had enough to do with this great house to keep in order, so many mouths to fill, and so many servants to oversee without wearing yourself out with nursing all Dr. Elliott's poor folks," I said gloomily.

"The more I have to do, the happier I am," she replied.

"Dear Katy, the old wound isn't healed yet, and I like to be with those who have wounds and bruises of their own. And Dr. Elliott seems to have divined this by instinct."

I ran and kissed her dear, pale face, which grows more beautiful every day. No wonder she misses Father so! He loved and honored her beyond description and never forgot one of those little courtesies that must have a great deal to do with a wife's happiness. People said of him that he was a gentleman of the old school, and that race is dying out.

I feel a good deal out of sorts myself. Oh, I do so wish to get above myself and all my childish, petty ways and to live in a region where there is no temptation and no sin!

April 20, 1836—

Yesterday I felt better than I have done since the accident. I ran about the house quite cheerily, for me. I wanted to see Mother for something and flew singing into the parlor, where I had left her shortly before. But she was not there, and Dr. Elliott was. I started back and was about to leave the room, but he detained me.

"Come in, I beg of you," he said, his voice growing hoarser and hoarser. "Let us put a stop to this."

"To what?" I asked, going nearer and nearer and looking up into his face, which was quite pale.

"To your evident terror of being alone with me, of hearing me speak. Let me assure you, once for all, that nothing would tempt me to annoy you by urging myself upon you, as you seem to fear I may be tempted to do. I cannot force you to love me nor would I if I could. If you ever want a friend, you will find one in me. But do not think of me as your lover or treat me as if I were always lying in wait for a chance to remind you of it. That I shall never do, never."

"Oh, no, of course not!" I broke forth, my face all in a glow and tears of mortification raining down my cheeks. "I knew you did not care for me! I knew you had got over it!"

I don't know which of us began it; I don't think he did and I am sure I did not, but the next moment I was folded all up in his great long arms, and a new life had begun!

Mother opened the door not long after and, seeing what was going on, trotted away on her dear old feet as fast as she could.

APRIL 21—

I am too happy to write journals. To think how we love each other!

Mother behaves beautifully.

APRIL 25—

One does not feel like saying much about it when one is as happy as I am. I walk the street as one treading on air. I fly about the house as on wings. I kiss everybody I see.

Now that I look at Ernest (for he makes me call him so) with unprejudiced eyes, I wonder I ever thought him clumsy. And how ridiculous it was in me to confound his dignity and manliness with age!

It is very odd, however, that such a cautious, well-balanced man should have fallen in love with me that day at Sunday school. And still stranger that with my headlong, impulsive nature I deliberately walked into love with him!

I believe we shall never get through with what we

have to say to each other. I am afraid we are rather selfish to leave Mother to herself every evening.

JAN. 16, 1837—

Yesterday was my birthday and today is my wedding day. We meant to celebrate the one with the other, but Sunday would come this year on the fifteenth.

I am dressed and have turned everybody out of this room, where I have suffered so much mortification and experienced so much joy, that before I give myself to Ernest and before I leave home forever, I may once more give myself away to God. I have been too much absorbed in my earthly love and am shocked to find how it fills my thoughts. But I will belong to God. I will begin my married life in His fear, depending on Him to make me an unselfish, devoted wife.

JAN. 25—

We had a delightful trip after the wedding was over. Ernest proposed to take me to his own home that I might see his mother and sister. He never has said that he wanted them to see me, but his mother is not well. I am heartily glad of it. I mean, I was glad to escape going there to be examined and criticized. Every one of them would pick at me, I am sure, and I don't like to be picked at.

We have a home of our own, and I am trying to take kindly to housekeeping. Ernest is away a great deal more than I expected he would be. I am fearfully lonely. Aunty comes to see me as often as she can, and I go there almost every day, but that doesn't amount to much. As soon as I can venture to do it, I shall ask Ernest to let me invite Mother to come and live with us. It is not right for her to be left alone so. I hoped he would do that himself. But men are not like women. We think of everything.

FEB. 17—

Mrs. Embury has been here today. I longed to compare notes with her and find out whether it really is my fault that I am not quite happy. But I could not bear to open my heart to her on so sacred a subject. We had some general conversation, however, which did me good for the time, at least.

She said she thought one of the first lessons a wife should learn is self-forgetfulness. I wondered if she had seen anything in me to call forth this remark. We meet pretty often, partly because our husbands are such good friends, partly because she is as fond of music as I am; and we like to sing and play together, and I never see her that she does not do or say something elevating, something that strengthens my own best purposes and desires. But she knows nothing of my conflict and dismay and never will. Her gentle nature responds at once to holy influences. I feel truly grateful to her for loving me, for she really does love me, and yet she must see my faults.

I should like to know if there is any reason on earth why a woman should learn self-forgetfulness that does not involve a man?

FEB. 24—

Ernest has been gone a week. His mother is worse and he had to go. I wanted to go, too, but he said it was not worthwhile, as he should have to return directly. Dr. Embury takes charge of his patients during his absence, and Mrs. E. and Aunty and the children come to see me very often. I like Mrs. Embury more and more. She is not so audacious as I am, but I believe she agrees with me more than she will own.

FEB. 25—

Ernest writes that his mother is dangerously ill and seems in great distress. I am mean enough to want all his love myself, while I should hate him if he gave none to her. Poor Ernest! If she should die, he would be sadly afflicted!

FEB. 27—

She died the very day he wrote. How I long to fly to him and to comfort him! I can think of nothing else. I pray day and night that God would make me a better wife.

A letter came from Mother at the same time with Ernest's. She evidently misses me more than she will own. Just as soon as Ernest returns home, I will ask him to let her come and live with us. I am sure he will; he loves her already; and now that his mother has gone, he will find her a real comfort. I am sure she will only make our home happier.

MARCH 10—

Things are even worse than I expected [since Ernest's father and sister Martha came to live with us]. Ernest evidently looked at me with his father's eyes (and his father has got the jaundice or something) and certainly is cooler toward me than he was before he went home. Martha still declines eating more than enough to keep body and soul together and sits at the table with the air of a martyr. Her father lives on crackers and stewed prunes; and when he has eaten them, fixes his melancholy eyes on me, watching every mouthful with an air of plaintive regret that I will consume so much unwholesome food.

Then Ernest positively spends less time with me than ever and sits in his office reading and writing nearly every evening.

Yesterday I came home from an exhilarating walk and a charming call at Aunty's and at the dinner table gave a lively account of some of the children's exploits. Nobody laughed, and nobody made any response; and after dinner Ernest took me aside and said, kindly enough, but still said it, "My little wife must be careful how she runs on in my father's presence. He has great dread of everything that might be thought levity."

Then all the vials of my wrath exploded and went off. . . .

MARCH 20—

I have had such a truly beautiful letter today from dear Mother! She gives up the hope of coming to spend her last years with us with a sweet patience that makes me cry whenever I think of it. What is the secret of this instant and cheerful consent to whatever God wills? Oh, that I had it, too! She begs me to be considerate and kind to Ernest's father and sister and constantly remind myself that my Heavenly Father has chosen to give me this care and trial on the very threshold of my married life. I am afraid I have quite lost sight of that in my indignation with Ernest for bringing them here.

NOVEMBER 6—

Aunty has put me in the way of doing that [helping Ernest pay his Father's debts]. I could not tell her the whole story, of course, but I made her understand that Ernest needed money for a generous purpose and that I wanted to help him in it. She said the children needed both music and drawing lessons and that she should be delighted if I would take them in hand. Aunty does not care a fig for accomplishments, but I think I am right in accepting her offer, as the children ought to learn to sing and to play and to draw. Of course I cannot have them come here, as Ernest's father could not bear the noise they would make; besides, I want to take Ernest by surprise and keep the whole thing a secret.

Nov. 14—

I have seen by the way Martha draws down the corners of her mouth of late that I am unusually out of favor with her. This evening, Ernest, coming home quite late, found me lolling back in my chair, idling after a hard day's work with my little cousins and Martha sewing nervously away at the rate of ten knots an hour, which is the first pun I ever made.

"Why will you sit up and sew at such a rate, Martha?" he asked.

She twitched at her thread, broke it, and began with a new one before she replied.

"I suppose you find it convenient to have a whole shirt to your back."

I saw then that she was making his shirts! It made me both hot and cold at once. What must Ernest think of me?

It is plain enough what he thinks of her, for he said, quite warmly for him, "This is really too kind."

What right has she to prowl round among Ernest's things and pry into the state of his wardrobe? If I had not had my time so broken up giving lessons, I should have found out that he needed new shirts and set to work on them. Though I must own I hate shirt making. I could not help showing that I felt aggrieved. Martha defended herself by saying that she knew young people would be young people and would gad about, shirts or no shirts. Now it is not her fault that she thinks I waste my time gadding about, but I am just as angry with her as if it were. Oh, why couldn't I have had Helen to be a pleasant companion and friend to me instead of this old—well, I won't say what.

And really, with so much to make me happy, what would become of me if I had no trials?

Nov. 18—

Oh, I am so happy that I sing for joy! Dear Ernest has given me such a delightful surprise! He says he has persuaded James to come and spend his college days here and finally study medicine with him. Dear, darling old James! He is to be here tomorrow. He is to have the little hall bedroom fitted up for him, and he will be here several years. Next to having Mother, this is the nicest thing that could happen. We love each other so dearly and get along so beautifully together. I wonder how he'll like Martha with her grim ways and Ernest's father with his melancholy ones.

DECEMBER 7—

James is my perpetual joy and pride. We read and sing together, just as we used to do in our old schooldays. Martha sits by with her work, grimly approving; for is he not a man? And, as if my cup of felicity were not full enough, I am to have my dear old pastor come here to settle over this church, and I shall once more hear his beloved voice in the pulpit. Ernest has managed the whole thing. He says the state of Dr. C.'s health makes the change quite necessary and that he can avail himself of the best surgical advice this city affords, in case his old difficulties recur. I rejoice for myself and for this church, but Mother will miss him sadly.

I am leading a very busy, happy life; only I am, perhaps, working a little too hard. What with my scholars, the extra amount of housework Martha contrives to get out of me, the practicing I must keep up if I am to teach, and the many steps I have to take, I have not only no idle moments, but none too many for recreation. Ernest is so busy himself that he fortunately does not see what a race I am running.

JANUARY 16, 1838—

The first anniversary of our wedding day and, like all days, has had its lights and its shades. I thought I would celebrate it in such a way as to give pleasure to everybody and spent a good deal of time in getting up a little gift for each from Ernest and myself. And I took special pains to have a good dinner, particularly for Father. Yes, I had made up my mind to call him by that sacred name for this first time today, cost what it may. But he shut himself up in his room directly after breakfast and, when dinner was ready, refused to come down. This cast a gloom over us all. Then Martha was nearly distracted because a valuable dish has been broken in the kitchen, and she could not recover her equanimity at all. Worst of all, Ernest, who is not in the least sentimental, never said a word about our wedding day and didn't give me a thing! I have kept hoping all day that he would make me some little present, no matter how small, but now it is too late; he has gone out to be gone all night, probably, and thus ends the day, an utter failure.

I feel a good deal disappointed. Besides, when I look back over this, my first year of married life, I do not feel satisfied with myself at all. I can't help feeling that I have been selfish and unreasonable toward Ernest in a great many ways and as contrary to have felt a good deal of secret contempt for his father, with his moods and tenses, his pillboxes and his plasters, his feastings and his fastings. I do not understand how a Christian can make such slow progress as I do and how old faults can hang on so.

If I had made any real progress, should I not be sensible of it?

I have been reading over the early part of this journal, and when I came to the conversation I had with Mrs. Cabot, in which I made a list of my wants, I was astonished that I could ever have had such contemptible ones. Let me think what I really and truly most want now.

First of all, then, if God should speak to me at this moment and offer to give just one thing and that alone, I should say without hesitation, Love to Thee, O my Master!

Next to that, if I could have one thing more, I would choose to be a thoroughly unselfish, devoted wife. Down in my secret heart I know there lurks another wish, which I am ashamed of. It is that in some way or other, some right way, I could be delivered from Martha and her father. I shall never be any better while they are here to tempt me!

FEBRUARY 1—

Ernest spoke today of one of his patients, a Mrs. Campbell, who is a great sufferer but whom he describes as the happiest, most cheerful person he ever met. He rarely speaks of his patients. Indeed, he rarely speaks of anything. I felt strangely attracted by what he said of her and asked so many questions that at last he proposed to take me to see her. I caught at the idea very eagerly and have just come home from the visit greatly moved and touched. She is confined to her bed and is quite helpless, and at times her sufferings are terrible. She received me with a sweet smile, however, and led me on to talk more of myself than I ought to have done. I wish Ernest had not left me alone with her so that I should have had the restraint of his presence.

MARCH 1—

Aunty sent for us all to dine with her today to celebrate Lucy's fifteenth birthday. Ever since Lucy behaved so heroically in regard to little Emma, really saving her life, Ernest says, Aunty seems to feel that she cannot do enough for her. The child has taken the most unaccountable fancy to me, strangely enough, and when we got there she came to meet me with something like cordiality.

"Mamma permits me to be the bearer of agreeable news," she said, "because this is my birthday. A friend of whom you are very fond has just arrived and is impatient to embrace you."

"To embrace me?" I cried. "You foolish child!" And the next moment I found myself in my mother's arms!

The despised Lucy had been the means of giving this pleasure. It seems that Aunty had told her she should choose her own birthday treat and that after solemn meditation, she had decided that to see dear Mother again would be the most agreeable thing she could think of. I have never told you, dear Journal, why I did not go home last summer and never shall. If you choose to fancy that I couldn't afford it, you can!

Well! Wasn't it nice to see Mother and to read in her dear, loving face that she was satisfied with her poor, wayward Katy and fond of her as ever! I only longed for Ernest's coming, that she might see us together and see how he loved me.

He came; I rushed out to meet him and dragged him in. But it seemed as if he had grown stupid and awkward. All through the dinner I watched for one of those loving glances that would proclaim to Mother the good understanding between us, but I watched in vain.

"It will come by and by," I thought. "When we get by ourselves, Mother will see how fond of me he is." But "by and by" it was just the same. I was preoccupied, and Mother asked me if I were well. It was all very foolish, I daresay, and yet I did want to have her know that with all my faults he still loves me. Then, besides the disappointment, I have to reproach myself for misunderstanding poor Lucy as I have done. Because she was not all fire and fury like myself, I need not have assumed that she had no heart. It is just like me; I hope I shall never be so severe in my judgment again.

APRIL 30—

Mother has just gone. Her visit has done me a world of good. She found out something to like in Father at once and then something good in Martha. She says Father's sufferings are real, not fancied, that his error is not knowing where to locate his disease, and is starving one week and overeating the next. She charged me not to lay up future misery for myself by misjudging him now and to treat him as a daughter ought without the smallest regard to his appreciation of it. Then as to Martha, she declares that I have no idea how much she does to reduce our expenses, to keep the house in order, and relieve us from care. "But, Mother," I said, "did you notice what horrid butter we have? And it is all her doing."

"But the butter won't last forever," she replied. "Don't make yourself miserable about such a trifle. For my part, it is a great relief to me to know that with your delicate health you have this tower of strength to lean on."

"But my health is not delicate, Mother."

"You certainly look pale and thin."

"Oh, well," I said, whereupon she fell to giving me all sorts of advice about getting up on stepladders, and climbing on chairs, and sewing too much, and all that.

JUNE 15—

The weather, or something, makes me rather languid and stupid. I begin to think that Martha is not an entire nuisance in the house. I have just been to see Mrs. Campbell. In answer to my routine lamentations, she took up a book and read me what was called, as nearly as I can remember, "Four steps that lead to peace."

"Be desirous of doing the will of another, rather than thine own."

"Choose always to have less, rather than more."

"Seek always the lowest place and to be inferior to everyone."

"Wish always, and pray, that the will of God may be wholly fulfilled in thee."

I was much struck with these directions; but I said despondently, "If peace can only be found at the end of such hard roads, I am sure I shall always be miserable."

"Are you miserable now?" she asked.

"Yes, just now I am. I do not mean that I have no happiness; I mean that I am in a disheartened mood, weary of going round and round in circles, committing the same sins, uttering the same confessions, and making no advance."

"My dear," she said after a time, "have you a perfectly distinct, settled view of what Christ is to the human soul?"

"I do not know. I understand, of course, more or less perfectly that my salvation depends on Him alone; it is His gift."

"But do you see with equal clearness that your sanctification must be as fully His gift as your salvation is?"

"No," I said after a little thought. "I have had a feeling that He has done His part and now I must do mine."

"My dear," she said with much tenderness and feeling, "then the first thing you have to do is to learn Christ."

"But how?"

"On your knees, my child, on your knees!" She was tired, and I came away; and I have indeed been on my knees.

July 1—

I think that I do begin, dimly, it is true, but really, to understand that this terrible work that I was trying to do myself is Christ's work and must be done and will be done by Him. I take some pleasure in the thought and wonder why it has all this time been hidden from me, especially after what Dr. C. said in his letter. But I get hold of this idea in a misty, unsatisfactory way. If Christ is to do all, what am I to do? And have I been told over and over again that the Christian life is one of conflict and that I am to fight like a good soldier?

August 5—

Dr. Cabot has come just as I need him most. I long for one of those good talks with him that always used to strengthen me so. I feel a perfect weight of depression that makes me a burden to myself and to poor Ernest, who, after visiting sick people all day, needs to come home to a cheerful wife. But he comforts me with the assurance that this is merely physical despondency and that I shall get over it by and by. How kind, how even tender, he is! My heart is getting all it wants from him; only I am too stupid to enjoy him as I ought. Father, too, talks far less about his own bad feelings and seems greatly concerned at mine. As to Martha, I have done trying to get sympathy or love from her. She cannot help it, I suppose, but she is very hard and dry toward me; and I feel such a longing to throw myself on her mercy and to have one little smile to assure me that she has forgiven me for being Ernest's wife and so different from what she would have chosen for him.

Dr. Elliott to Mrs. Mortimer:

October 4, 1838
My dear Katy's Mother: You will rejoice with us when I tell you that we are the happy parents of a very fine little boy. My dearest wife sends "an ocean of love" to you and says she will write herself tomorrow. That I shall not be very likely to allow, as you will imagine. She is doing extremely well, and we have everything to be grateful for.

Your affectionate Son,
J. E. Elliott

Nov. 4—

My darling baby is a month old today. I never saw such a splendid child. I love him so that I lie awake nights to watch him. Martha says, in her dry way, that I had better show my love by sleeping and eating for him, and Ernest says I shall as soon as I get stronger. But I don't get strong, and that discourages me.

Nov. 26—

I begin to feel rather more myself and as if I could write with less labor. I have had in these few past weeks such a revelation of suffering and such a revelation of joy as mortal mind can hardly conceive of. The world I live in now is a new world, a world full of suffering that leads to unutterable felicity. Oh, this precious, precious baby! How can I thank God enough for giving him to me!

I see now why He has put some thorns into my domestic life; but for them I should be too happy to live. It does now seem just the moment to complain, and yet, as I can speak to no one, it is a relief, a great relief, to write about my trials. During my whole sickness, Martha has been so hard, so cold, so unsympathizing that sometimes it has seemed as if my cup of trial could not hold another drop. She routed me out of bed when I was so languid that everything seemed a burden and when sitting up made me faint away. I heard her say to herself that I had no constitution and had no business to be married. The worst of all is that during that dreadful night before baby came, she kept asking Ernest to lie down and rest and was sure he would kill himself and all that, while she had not one word of pity for me. But, oh, why need I let this rankle in my heart! Why cannot I turn my thoughts entirely to my darling baby, my dear husband, and all the other sources of joy that make my home a happy one in spite of this one discomfort! I hope I am learning some useful lessons from my joys and from my trials, and that both will serve to make me in earnest and to keep me so.

JANUARY 16, 1839—

This is our second wedding day. I did not expect much from it after last year's failure. Father was very gloomy at breakfast and retired to his room directly after it. No one could get in to make his bed, and he would not come down to dinner. I wonder Ernest lets him go on so. But his rule seems to be to let everybody have their own way. He certainly lets me have mine. After dinner he gave me a book I have been wanting for some time and had asked him for—*The Imitation of Christ*. Ever since that day at

Mrs. Campbell's, I have felt that I should like it, though I did think, in old times, that it preached too hard a doctrine. I read aloud to him the "Four steps to peace"; he said they were admirable and then took it from me and began reading to himself here and there. I felt the precious moments when I had got him all to myself were passing away and was becoming quite out of patience with him when the words, "Constantly seek to have less, rather than more," flashed into my mind. I suppose this direction had reference to worldly goods, but I despise money and despise people who love it. The riches I crave are not silver and gold, but my husband's love and esteem. And of these must I desire to have less rather than more? I puzzled myself over this question in vain, but when I silently prayed to be satisfied with just what God chose to give me of the wealth I crave, yes, hunger and thirst for, I certainly felt a sweet content, for the time at least, that was quite resting and quieting. And just as I had reached that acquiescent mood, Ernest threw down his book and came and caught me in his arms.

"I thank God," he said, "my precious wife, that I married you this day. The wisest thing I ever did was when I fell in love with you and made a fool of myself!"

What a speech for my silent old darling to make! Whenever he says and does a thing out of character and takes me all by surprise, how delightful he is! Now the world is a beautiful world, and so is everybody in it. I met Martha on the stairs after Ernest had gone and caught her and kissed her. She looked perfectly astonished.

"What spirits the child has!" I heard her whisper to herself. "No sooner down than up again."

And she sighed. Can it be that under that stern and hard crust, there lie hidden affections and perhaps hidden sorrows?

I ran back and asked as kindly as I could, "What makes you sigh, Martha? Is anything troubling you? Have I done anything to annoy you?"

"You do the best you can," she said and pushed past me to her own room.

Feb. 25—

Things have not gone on well of late. Dearly as I love Ernest, he has lowered himself in my eye by telling that [about his father's debt] to Dr. Cabot. It would have been far nobler to be silent concerning his sacrifices; and he certainly grows harder, graver, sterner, every day. He is all shut up within himself, and I am growing afraid of him. It must be that he is bitterly disappointed in me and takes refuge in this awful silence. Oh, if I could only please him and could know that I pleased him, how different my life would be!

Baby does not seem well. I have often plumed myself on the thought that having a doctor for his father would be such an advantage to him, as he would be ready to attack the first symptoms of disease. But Ernest hardly listens to me when I express anxiety about this or that; and if I ask a question he replies, "Oh, you know better than I do. Mothers know by instinct how to manage babies." But I do not know by instinct or in any other way, and I often wish that the time I spent over my music had been spent in learning how to meet all the little emergencies that are constantly arising since baby came. How I used to laugh in my sleeve at those anxious mothers who lived near us and always seemed to be in hot water. Martha will take baby when I have other things to attend to, and she keeps him every Sunday afternoon that I may go to church, but she knows no more about his physical training than I do. If my dear mother were only here! I feel a good deal worn-out. What with the care of baby, who is restless at night, and with whom I walk about lest he should keep Ernest awake, the depressing influence of Father's presence, Martha's disdain, and Ernest's keeping so aloof from me, life seems to me little better than a burden that I have not strength to carry and would gladly lay down.

MARCH 13—

If it were not for James, I believe I should sink. He is so kind and affectionate, so ready to fill up the gaps Ernest leaves empty, and is so sunshiny and gay that I cannot be entirely sad. Baby, too, is a precious treasure; it would be wicked to cloud his little life with my depression. I try to look to him always with a smiling face, for he already distinguishes between a cheerful and a sad countenance.

I am sure that there is something in Christ's gospel that would soothe and sustain me amid these varied trials if I only knew what it is and how to put forth my hand and take it. But as it is I feel very desolate. Ernest often congratulates me on having had such a good night's rest, when I have been up and down every hour with baby, half asleep and frozen and exhausted. But he shall sleep at any rate.

APRIL 5—

The first rays of spring make me more languid than ever. Martha cannot be made to understand that nursing such a large, voracious baby, losing sleep, and confinement within doors are enough to account for this. She is constantly speaking in terms of praise of those who keep up even when they do feel a little out of sorts and says she always does. In the evening, after baby goes to sleep, I feel fit for nothing but to lie on the sofa, dozing; but she sees in this only a lazy habit, which ought not to be tolerated and is constantly devising ways to rouse and set me at work. If I had more leisure for reading, meditation, and prayer, I might still be happy. But all the morning I must have baby till he takes his nap; and as soon as he gets to sleep, I must put my room in order; and by that time all the best part of the day is gone. And at night I am so tired that I can hardly feel anything but my weariness. That, too, is my only chance of seeing Ernest; and if I lock my door and fall upon my knees, I keep listening for his steps, ready to spring to welcome him should he come. This is wrong, I know, but how can I live without one loving word from him? And every day I am hoping it will come.

July 4—

Baby is ten months old today and in spite of everything is bright and well. I have come home to Mother. Ernest waked up at last to see that something must be done, and when he is awake he is very wide awake. So he brought me home. Dear Mother is perfectly delighted, only she will make an ado about my health. But I feel a good deal better and think I shall get nicely rested here. How pleasant it is to feel myself watched by friendly eyes, my faults excused and forgiven and what is best in me called out. I have been writing to Ernest and have told him honestly how annoyed and pained I was at learning that he had told his secret to Dr. Cabot.

AUGUST 1—

When I took leave of Ernest, I was glad to get away. I thought he would perhaps find after I was gone that he missed something out of his life and would welcome me home with a little of the old love. But I did not dream that he would not find it easy to do without me till summer was over; and when, this morning, he came suddenly upon us, carpetbag in hand, I could do nothing but cry in his arms like a tired child.

And now I had the silly triumph of having Mother see that he loved me!

"How could you get away?" I asked at last. "And what made you come? And how long can you stay?"

"I could get away because I would," he replied. "And I came because I wanted to come. And I can stay three days."

Three days of Ernest all to myself!

AUGUST 12—

I have had a long letter from Ernest today. He says he hopes he has not been selfish and unkind in speaking of his father and sister as he has done, because he truly loves and honors them both and wants me to do so, if I can. His father had called them up twice to see him die and to receive his last messages. This always happens when poor Ernest has been up all the previous night; there seems a fatality about it.

OCTOBER 4—

Home again and with my dear Ernest delighted to see me. Baby is a year old today, and, as usual, Father—who seems to abhor anything like a merrymaking—took himself off to his room. Tomorrow he will be all the worse for it and will be sure to have a theological battle with somebody.

MARCH 28, 1840—

It is almost six months since I wrote that. About the middle of October Father had one of his ill turns one night, and we were all called up. He asked for me particularly, and Ernest came for me at last. I was a good deal agitated and would not stop to half-dress myself; and as I had a slight cold already, I suppose I added to it then. At any rate I was taken very sick, and the worst cough I ever had has racked my poor frame almost to pieces. Nearly six months' confinement to my room; six months of uselessness during which I have been a mere cumberer of the ground. Poor Ernest! What a hard time he has had!

Instead of the cheerful welcome home I was to give him whenever he entered the house, here I have lain exhausted, woebegone, and good-for-nothing. It is the bitterest disappointment I ever had. My ambition is to be the sweetest, brightest, best of wives; and what with my childish follies and my sickness, what a weary life my dear husband has had! But how often I have prayed that God would do His will in defiance, if need be, of mine! I have tried to remind myself of that every day. But I am too tired to write any more now.

JUNE 20—

On the first of May there came to us, with other spring flowers, our little fair-haired, blue-eyed daughter. How rich I felt when I heard Ernest's voice, as he replied to a question asked at the door, proclaim, "Mother and children all well." To think that we who thought ourselves rich before are made so much richer now!

But she is not large and vigorous as little Ernest was, and we cannot rejoice in her without some misgiving. Yet her very frailty makes her precious to us. Little Ernest hangs over her with an almost loverlike pride and devotion; and should she live, I can imagine what a protector he will be for her. I have had to give up the care of him to Martha. During my illness, I do not know what would have become of him but for her. One of the pleasant events of every day at that time was her bringing him to me in such exquisite order, his face shining with health and happiness, his hair and dress so beautifully neat and clean. Now that she has the care of him, she has become very fond of him; and he certainly forms one bond of union between us, for we both agree that he is the handsomest, best, most remarkable child that ever lived or ever will live.

JULY 6—

I have come home to dear Mother with both my children. Ernest says our only hope for baby is to keep her out of the city during the summer months.

What a petite wee maiden she is. Where does all the love come from? If I had had her always, I do not see how I could be more fond of her. And do people call it living who never had any children?

AUGUST—

Dear Ernest has come to spend a week with us. He is all tired out, as there has been a great deal of sickness in the city, and Father has had quite a serious attack. He brought with him a nurse for baby as one more desperate effort to strengthen her constitution.

I reproached him for doing it without consulting me, but he said Mother had written to tell him that I was worn-out and not in a state to have the care of the children. It has been a terrible blow to me. One by one I am giving up the sweetest maternal duties. God means that I shall be nothing and do nothing, a mere useless sufferer. But when I tell Ernest so, he says I am everything to him and that God's children please Him just as well when they sit patiently with folded hands, if that is His will, as when they are hard at work. But to be at work, to be useful, to be necessary to my husband and children is just what I want; and I do find it hard to be set against the wall, as it were, like an old piece of furniture no longer of any service. I see now that my first desire has not been to please God but to please myself, for I am restless under His restraining hand and find my prison a very narrow one. I would be willing to bear any other trial if I could only have health and strength for my beloved ones. I pray for patience with bitter tears.

OCTOBER—

We are all home together once more. The parting with Mother was very painful. Every year that she lives now increases her loneliness and makes me long to give her the shelter of my home. But in the midst of these anxieties, how much I have to make me happy! Little Ernest is the life and soul of the house; the sound of his feet pattering about and all his prattle are the sweetest music to my ear; and his heart is brimful of love and joy so that he shines on us all like a sunbeam. Baby is improving every day and is one of those tender, clinging things that appeal to everybody's love and sympathy. I never saw a more angelic face than hers. Father sits by the hour looking at her. Today he said:

"Daughter Katherine, this lovely little one is not meant for this sinful world."

"This world needs to be adorned with lovely little ones," I said. "And baby was never so well as she is now."

"Do not set your heart too fondly upon her," he returned. "I feel that she is far too dear to me."

"But, Father, we could give her to God if He should ask for her. Surely we love Him better than we love her."

But as I spoke, a sharp pang shot through and through my soul, and I held my little fair daughter closely in my arms as if I could always keep her there. It may be conceit, but it really does seem as if poor Father was getting a little fond of me. Ever since my own sickness, I have felt great sympathy for him; and he feels, no doubt, that I give him something neither Ernest nor Martha can do, since they were never sick one day in their lives. I do wish he could look more at Christ and at what He has done and is doing for us. The way of salvation is to me a wide path, absolutely radiant with the glory of Him who shines upon it. I see my shortcomings; I see my sins; but I feel myself bathed, as it were, in the effulgent glow that proceeds directly from the throne of God and the Lamb. It seems as if I ought to have some misgivings about my salvation, but I can hardly say that I have one. How strange, how mysterious that is! And here is Father, so much older, so much better than I am, creeping along in the dark! I spoke to Ernest about it. He says I owe it to my training, in a great measure, and that my mother is fifty years in advance of her age. But it can't be all that. It was only after years of struggle and prayer that God gave me this joy.

JAN. 16, 1841—

One more desperate effort to make harmony out of the discords of my house and one more failure. Ernest forgot that it was our wedding day, which mortified and pained me, especially as he had made an engagement to dine out. I am always expecting something from life that I never get. Is it so with everybody? I am very uneasy, too, about James. He seems to be growing fond of Lucy's society. I am perfectly sure that she could not make him happy. Is it possible that he does not know what a brilliant young man he is and that he can have whom he pleases? It is easy, in theory, to let God plan our own destiny and that of our friends. But when it comes to a specific case, we fancy we can help His judgment with our poor reason. Well, I must go to Him with this new anxiety and trust my darling brother's future to Him, if I can.

I shall try to win James's confidence. If it is not Lucy, who or what is it that is making him thoughtful and serious yet so wondrously happy?

JAN. 17—

I have been trying to find out whether this is a mere notion of mine about Lucy. James laughs and evades my questions. But he owns that a very serious matter is occupying his thoughts, of which he does not wish to speak at present. May God bless him in it, whatever it is!

MAY 1—

My delicate little Una's first birthday. Thank God for sparing her to us a year. If He should take her away, I should still rejoice that this life was mingled with ours and has influenced us. Yes, even an unconscious infant is an ever-felt influence in the household. What an amazing thought!

I have given this precious little one away to her Savior and to mine; living or dying, she is His.

DEC. 13—

Writing journals does not seem to be my mission on earth of late. My busy hands find so much else to do! And sometimes when I have been particularly exasperated and tried by the jarring elements that form my home, I have not dared to indulge myself with recording things that ought to be forgotten.

How I long to live in peace with everyone, and how I resent interference in the management of my children! If the time ever comes that I live, a spinster of a certain age in the family of an elder brother, what a model of forbearance, charity, and sisterly loving-kindness I shall be!

JAN. 2, 1842—

James means to study theology as well as medicine, it seems. That will keep him with us for some years. Oh, is it selfish to take this view of it? Alas, the spirit is willing to have him go, but the flesh is weak and cries out.

MARCH 20—

I have been much impressed by Dr. Cabot's sermons today. While I am listening to his voice and hear him speak of the beauty and desirableness of the Christian life, I feel as he feels—that I am willing to count all things but dross that I may win Christ. But when I come home to my worldly cares, I get completely absorbed in them; and it is only by a painful wrench that I force my soul back to God. Sometimes I almost envy Lucy her calm nature, which gives her so little trouble. Why need I throw my whole soul into whatever I do? Why can't I make so much as an apron for little Ernest without ardor and eagerness of a soldier marching to battle? I wonder if people of my temperament ever get toned down and learn to take life coolly?

JUNE 10—

My dear little Una has had a long and very severe illness. It seems wonderful that she could survive such sufferings. And it is almost as wonderful that I could look upon them week after week without losing my senses.

At first Ernest paid little attention to my repeated entreaties that he would prescribe for her, and some precious time was thus lost. But the moment he was fully aroused to see her danger, there was something beautiful in his devotion. He often walked the room with her by the hour together, and it was touching to see her lying like a pale, crushed lily in his strong arms. One morning she seemed almost gone, and we knelt around her with bursting hearts to commend her parting soul to Him in whose arms we were about to place her. But it seemed as if all He asked of us was to come to that point, for then He gave her back to us; and she is still ours, only sevenfold dearer. I was so thankful to see dear Ernest's faith triumphing over his heart and making him so ready to give up even his lamb without a word. Yes, we will give our children to Him if He asks for them. He shall never have to snatch them from us by force.

OCT. 4—

We have had a quiet summer in the country; that is, I have with my darling little ones. This is the fourth birthday of our son and heir, and he has been full of health and vivacity, enjoying everything with all his heart. How he lights up our somber household! Father has been fasting today and is worn-out and so nervous in consequence that he could not bear the sound of the children's voices. I wish, if he must fast, he would do it moderately and do it all the time. Now he goes without food until he is ready to sink, and now he eats quantities of improper food. If Martha could only see how mischievous all this is for him. After the children had been hustled out of the way and I had got them both off to bed, he said in his most doleful manner, "I hope, my daughter, that you are faithful to your son. He has now reached the age of four years and is a remarkably intelligent child. I hope you teach him that he is a sinner and that he is in a state of condemnation."

"No, Father, don't," I said. "You are all tired out and do not know what you are saying. I would not have little Ernest hear you for the world."

Poor Father! He fairly groaned.

"You are responsible for the child's soul," he said. "You have more influence over him than all the world beside."

"I know it," I said, "and sometimes I feel ready to sink when I think of the great work God has entrusted to me.

But my poor child will learn that he is a sinner only too soon; and before that dreadful day arrives, I want to fortify his soul with the only antidote against the misery that knowledge will give him. I want him to see his Redeemer in all His love and all His beauty and to love Him with all his heart and soul and mind and strength. Dear Father, pray for him, and pray for me, too."

"I do; I will," he said solemnly. And then followed the inevitable long fit of silent musing, when I often wonder what is passing in that suffering soul. For a sufferer he certainly is who sees a great and good and terrible God who cannot look upon iniquity and does not see His risen Son, who has paid the debt we owe, and lives to intercede for us before the throne of the Father.

NOVEMBER—

This morning Ernest received an early summons to Amelia. I got out of all manner of patience with him because he would take his bath and eat his breakfast before he went and should have driven anyone else distracted by my hurry and flurry.

"She has had a hemorrhage!" I cried. "Do, Ernest, make haste."

"Of course," he returned, "that would come sooner or later."

"You don't mean," I said, "that she has been in danger of this all along?"

"I certainly do."

"Then it was very unkind in you not to tell me so."

"I told you at the outset that her lungs were diseased."

"No, you told me no such thing. Oh, Ernest, is she going to die?"

"I did not know you were so fond of her," he said apologetically.

"It is not that," I cried. "I am distressed at the thought of the worldly life she has been living—at my never trying to influence her for her good. If she is in danger, you will tell her so? Promise me that."

"I must see her before I make such a promise," he said and went out.

I flew up to my room and threw myself on my knees, sorrowful, self-condemned. I had thrown away my last opportunity of speaking a word to her in season, though I had seen how much she needed one, and now she was going to die! Oh, I hope God will forgive me and hear the prayers I have offered for her!

EVENING—

Ernest says he had a most distressing scene at Amelia's this morning. She insisted on knowing what he thought of her and then burst into bitter complaints and lamentations, charging it to her husband that she had this disease, declaring that she could not and would not die, and insisting that he must prevent it. Her uncle urged for a consultation of physicians, to which Ernest consented, of course, though he says no mortal power can save her now. I asked him how her husband appeared, to which he made the evasive answer that he appeared just as one would expect him to do.

JAN. 18, 1843—

Our wedding day has passed unobserved. Amelia's suffering condition absorbs us all. Martha spends much time with her and prepares almost all the food she eats.

MARCH 1—

Poor Amelia's short race on earth is over. Dr. Cabot saw her every few days and says he hopes she did depart in Christian faith, though without Christian joy. I have not seen her since that last interview. That excited me so that Ernest would not let me go again.

Martha has been there nearly the whole time for three or four weeks, and I really think it has done her good. She seems less absorbed in mere outside things and more lenient toward me and my failings.

I do not know what is to become of those motherless little girls. I wish I could take them into my own home, but, of course, that is not even to be thought of at this juncture. Ernest says their father seemed nearly distracted when Amelia died and that his uncle is going to send him off to Europe immediately.

I have been talking with Ernest about Amelia. "What do you think," I asked, "about her last days on earth? Was there really any preparation for death?"

"These scenes are very painful," he returned. "Of course there is but one real preparation for Christian dying, and that is Christian living."

"But the sickroom often does what a prosperous life never did!"

"Not often. Sick persons delude themselves or are deluded by their friends; they do not believe they are really about to die. Besides, they are bewildered and exhausted by disease; and what mental strength they have is occupied with studying symptoms, watching for the doctor, and the like. I do not now recall a single instance where a worldly Christian died a happy, joyful death, in all my patients."

"Well, in one sense it makes no difference whether

they die happily or not. The question is, do they die in the Lord?"

"It may make no vital difference to them; but we must not forget that God is honored or dishonored by the way a Christian dies as well as by the way in which he lives. There is great significance in the description given in the Bible of the death by which John should 'glorify God' (John 21:19); to my mind it implies that to die well is to live well."

"But how many thousands die suddenly or of such exhausting disease that they cannot honor God by even one feeble word?"

"Of course I do not refer to such cases. All I ask is that those whose minds are clear, who are able to attend to all other final details should let it be seen what the gospel of Christ can do for poor sinners in the great exigency of life, giving Him the glory. I can tell you, my darling, that standing, as I so often do, by dying beds, this whole subject has become one of great magnitude to my mind. And it gives me positive personal pain to see heirs of the eternal kingdom, made such by the ignominious death of their Lord, go shrinking and weeping to the full possession of their inheritance."

Ernest is right, I am sure; but how shall the world, even the Christian world, be convinced that it may have blessed foretastes of heaven while yet plodding upon earth and faith to go thither joyfully for the simple asking?

Poor Amelia! But she understands it all now. It is a blessed thing to have this great faith, and it is a blessed thing to have a Savior who accepts it when it is but a mere grain of mustard seed!

MAY 24—

I celebrated my little Una's third birthday by presenting her with a new brother. Both the children welcomed him with delight that was of itself compensation enough for all it cost me to get up such a celebration. Martha takes a most prosaic view of this proceeding, in which she detects malice prepense on my part. She says I shall now have one mouth the more to fill and two feet the more to shoe, more disturbed nights, more laborious days, and less leisure or visiting, reading, music, and drawing.

Well! This is one side of the story, to be sure, but I look at the other. Here is a sweet, fragrant mouth to kiss; here are two more feet to make music with their pattering about my nursery. Here is a soul to train for God; and the body in which it dwells is worthy of all it will cost, since it is the abode of a kingly tenant. I may see less of friends, but I have gained one dearer than them all, to whom, while I minister in Christ's name, I make a willing sacrifice of what little leisure for my own recreation my other darlings had left me.

Yes, my precious baby, you are welcome to your mother's heart, welcome to her time, her strength, her health, her tenderest cares, to her lifelong prayers! Oh, how rich I am, how truly, how wondrously blest!

JUNE 21—

It seems that the happy man who has wooed Martha and won her is no less a personage than old Mr. Underhill, Amelia's uncle. His ideal of a woman is one who has no nerves, no sentiment, no backaches, no headaches, who will see that the wheels of his household machinery are kept well oiled, so that he need never hear them creak and who, in addition to her other accomplishments, believes in him and will be kind enough to live forever for his private accommodation. This exposé of his sentiments he has made to me in a loud, cheerful, pompous way; and he has also favored me with a description of his first wife, who lacked all these qualifications and was obliging enough to depart in peace at an early stage in their married life, meekly preferring thus to make way for a worthier successor. Mr. Underhill, with all his foibles, however, is on the whole a good man. He intends to take Amelia's little girls into his home and be a father, as Martha will be a mother, to them. For this reason he hurries on the marriage, after which they will all go at once to his country seat, which is easy of access and which he says he is sure Father will enjoy. Poor old Father! I hope he will; but when the subject is alluded to, he maintains a somber silence, and it seems to me he never spent so many days alone in his room, brooding over his misery, as he has of late. Oh, that I could comfort him.

OCTOBER 1—

I have had a charming summer with dear Mother; and now I have the great joy, so long deferred, of having her in my own home. Ernest has been very cordial about it, and James has settled up all her worldly affairs so that she has nothing to do now but to love us and let us love her. It is a pleasant picture to see her with my little darlings about her, telling the old sweet story she told me so often and making God and heaven and Christ such blissful realities. As I listen, I realize that it is to her I owe that early, deep-seated longing to please the Lord Jesus, which I never remember as having a beginning or an ending, though it did have its fluctuations. And it is another pleasant picture to see her sit in her own old chair, which Ernest was thoughtful enough to have brought for her, pondering cheerfully over her Bible and her Thomas à Kempis just as I have seen her do ever since I can remember. And there is still a third pleasant picture, only that is a new one; it is as she sits at my right hand at the table, the living personification of the blessed gospel of good tidings, with Father, opposite, the fading image of the law given by Moses. For Father has come back; Father and all his ailments, his pillboxes, his fits of despair, and his fits of dying. But he is quiet and gentle and even loving; and as he sits in his corner, his Bible on his knees, I see how much more he reads the New Testament than he used to do and that the fourteenth chapter of St. John almost opens to him of itself.

I must do Martha the justice to say that her absence, while it increases my domestic peace and happiness, increases my cares also. What with the children, the housekeeping, the thought for Mother's little comforts and the concern for Father's, I am like a bit of chaff driven before the wind and always in a hurry. There are so many stitches to be taken, so many things to pass through one's brain! Mother says no mortal woman ought to undertake so much, but what can I do? While Ernest is straining every nerve to pay off those debts, I must do all the needlework; and we must get along with servants whose want of skill makes them willing to put up with low wages. Of course I cannot tell Mother this, and I really believe she thinks I scrimp and pinch and overdo out of mere stinginess.

JAN. 1, 1844—

My mother says Ernest is entirely right in forbidding my working so hard. I must own that I already feel better. I have all the time I need to read my Bible and to pray now, and the children do not irritate and annoy me as they did. Who knows but I shall yet become quite amiable?

Ernest made his father very happy today by telling him that the last of those wretched debts is paid. I think that he might have told me that this deliverance was at hand. I did not know but we had years of these struggles with poverty before us. What with the relief from this anxiety, my improved state of health, and Father's pleasure, I am in splendid spirits today. Ernest, too, seems wonderfully cheerful, and we both feel that we may now look forward to a quiet happiness we have never known. With such a husband and such children as mine, I ought to be the most grateful creature on earth. And I have dear old Mother and James besides. I don't quite know what to think about James's relation to Lucy. He is so brimful and running over with happiness that he is also full of fun and of love, and after all he may only like her as a cousin.

FEB. 20—

Father grows weaker every day. Ernest has sent for his other children, John and Helen. Martha is no longer able to come here; her husband is very sick with a fever and cannot be left alone. No doubt he enjoys her bustling way of nursing and likes to have his pillows pushed from under him every five minutes. I am afraid I feel glad that she is kept away and that I have Father all to myself. Ernest never was so fond of me as he is now. I don't know what to make of it.

MARCH 1—

Father is very feeble and in great mental distress. He gropes about in the dark and shudders at the approach of death. We can do nothing but pray for him. And the cloud will be lifted when he leaves this world, if not before. For I know he is a good, yes, saintly man, dear to God and dear to Christ.

MARCH 4—

Dear Father has gone. We were all kneeling and praying and weeping around him when suddenly he called me to come to him. I went and let him lean his head on my breast as he loved to do. Sometimes I have stood so by the hour together ready to sink with fatigue and only kept up with the thought that if this were my own precious father's bruised head, I could stand and hold it forever.

"Daughter Katherine," he said in his faint, tremulous way, "you have come with me to the very brink of the river. I thank God for all your cheering words and ways. I thank God for giving you to be a helpmeet to my son. Farewell, now," he added in a low, firm voice. "I feel the bottom, and it is good!"

He lay back on his pillow, looking upward with an expression of seraphic peace and joy on his worn, meager face; and so his life passed gently away.

Oh, the affluence of God's payments! What a recompense for the poor love I had given my husband's father and the poor little services I had rendered him! Oh, that I had never been impatient with him, never smiled at his peculiarities, never in my secret heart felt him unwelcome to my home! And how wholly I overlooked, in my blind selfishness, what he must have suffered in feeling himself homeless, dwelling with us on sufferance, but master and head nowhere on earth! May God carry these lessons home to my heart of hearts and make this cloud of mingled remorse and shame that now envelopes me to descend in showers of love and benediction on every human soul that mine can bless!

APRIL—

I have had a new lesson that has almost broke my heart. In looking over his father's papers, Ernest found a little journal, brief in its records indeed; but we learn from it that on all those weddings and birthdays, when I fancied his austere religion made him hold aloof from our merry-making, he was spending the time in fasting and praying for us and for our children! Oh, shall I ever learn the sweet charity that thinketh no evil and believeth all things! What blessings may not have descended upon us and our children through those prayers! What evils may they not have warded off! Dear old Father! Oh, that I could once more put my loving arms about him and bid him welcome to our home! And how gladly would I now confess to him all my unjust judgments concerning him and entreat his forgiveness! Must life always go on thus? Must I always be erring, ignorant, and blind? How I hate this arrogant sweeping past my brother man, this utter ignoring of his hidden life!

I see now that it is well for Mother that she did not come to live with me at the beginning of my married life. I should not have borne with her little peculiarities nor have made her half so happy as I can now. I thank God that my varied disappointments and discomforts, my feeble health, my poverty, my mortifications have done me some little good and driven me to Him a thousand times because I could not get along without His help. But I am not satisfied with my state in His sight. I am sure something is lacking, though I know not what it is.

MAY—

Helen is going to stay here and live with Martha. How glad, how enchanted I am! Old Mr. Underhill is getting well; I saw him today. He can talk of nothing but his illness, of Martha's wonderful skill in nursing him, declaring that he owed his life to her. I felt a little piqued at this speech because Ernest was very attentive to him and no doubt did his share toward the cure. We have fitted up Father's room for a nursery. Hitherto all the children have had to sleep in our room, which has been bad for them and bad for us. I have been so afraid they would keep Ernest awake if they were unwell and restless. I have secured an excellent nurse, who is as fresh and blooming as the flower whose name she bears. The children are already attached to her, and I feel that the worst of my life is now over.

JUNE—

Little Ernest was taken sick on the very day I wrote that. The attack was fearfully sudden and violent. He is still very, very ill. I have not forgotten that I said once that I would give my children to God should He ask for them. And I will. But, oh, this agony of suspense! It eats into my soul and eats it away. Oh, my little Ernest! My firstborn son! My pride, my joy, my hope! And I thought the worst of my life was over!

OCT. 4—

My darling boy would have been six years old today. Ernest still keeps me shut up, but he rather urges my seeing a friend now and then. People say very strange things in the way of consolation. I begin to think that a tender clasp of the hand is about all one can give to the afflicted. One says I must not grieve because my child is better off in heaven. Yes, he is better off; I know it, I feel it, but I miss him nonetheless. Others say he might have grown up to be a bad man and broken my heart. Perhaps he might, but I cannot make myself believe that likely. One lady asked me if this affliction was not a rebuke of my idolatry of my darling; and another if I had not been in a cold, worldly state, needing this severe blow on that account.

But I find no consolation or support in these remarks. My comfort is in my perfect faith in the goodness and love of my Father, my certainty that He had a reason in thus afflicting me that I should admire and adore if I knew what it was. And in the midst of my sorrow I have had and do have a delight in Him hitherto unknown, so that sometimes this room in which I am a prisoner seems like the very gate of heaven.

MAY, 1845—

A long winter in my room and all sorts of painful remedies and appliances and deprivations. And now I am getting well and drive out every day. Martha sends her carriage, and Mother goes with me. Dear Mother! How nearly perfect she is! I never saw a sweeter face nor ever heard sweeter expressions of faith in God and love to all about her than hers. She has been my tower of strength all through these weary months, and yet she has shared my sorrow and made it her own.

I can see that Ernest's affliction and this prolonged anxiety about me have been a heavenly benediction to him. I am sure that every mother whose sick child he visits will have a sympathy he could not have given while all our own little ones were alive and well. I thank God that He has thus increased my dear husband's usefulness, as I think that He has mine also. How tenderly I already feel toward all suffering children, and how easy it will be now to be patient with them!

AUGUST 19—

I met today an old friend, Maria Kelly, who is married, it seems, and settled down in this pretty village [of Keene, New Hampshire]. She asked so many questions about my little Ernest that I had to tell her the whole story of his precious life, sickness, and death. I forced myself to do this quietly and without any great demand on her sympathies. My reward for the constraint I thus put upon myself was the abrupt question: "Haven't you grown stoical?"

I felt the angry blood rush through my veins as it has not done in a long time. My pride was wounded to the quick, and those cruel, unjust words still rankle in my heart. This is not as it should be. I am constantly praying that my pride may be humbled; and then when it is attacked, I shrink from the pain the blow causes and am angry with the hand that inflicts it. It is just so with two or three unkind things Martha has said to me. I can't help brooding over them and feeling stung with their injustice even while making the most desperate struggle to rise above and forget them. It is well for our fellow creatures that God forgives and excuses them when we fail to do it, and I can easily fancy that poor Maria Kelly is at this moment dearer in His sight than I am who have taken fire at a chance word. And I can see now, what I wonder I did not see at the time, that God was dealing very kindly and wisely with me when He made Martha overlook my good qualities, of which I suppose I have some, as everybody else has, and call out all my bad ones, since the ax was thus laid at the root of self-love. And it is plain that self-love cannot die without a fearful struggle.

May 26, 1846—

How long it is since I have written in my journal! We have had a winter full of cares, perplexities, and sicknesses. Mother began it by such a severe attack of inflammatory rheumatism as I could not have supposed she could live through. Her sufferings were dreadful, and I might almost say her patience was, for I often thought it would be less painful to hear her groan and complain than to witness such heroic fortitude, such sweet docility under God's hand. I hope I shall never forget the lessons I have learned in her sickroom. Ernest says he never shall cease to rejoice that she lives with us and that he can watch over her health. He has indeed been like a son to her, and this has been a great solace amid all her sufferings. Before she was able to leave the room, poor little Una was prostrated by one of her ill turns and is still very feeble. The only way in which she can be diverted is by reading to her, and I have done little else these two months but hold her in my arms, singing little songs and hymns, telling stories and reading what few books I find that are unexciting, simple, yet entertaining. My precious little darling! She bears the yoke in her youth without a frown, but it is agonizing to see her suffer so. How much easier it would be to bear all her physical infirmities myself! I suppose to those who look on from outside we must appear like a most unhappy family, since we hardly get free from one trouble before another steps in. But I see more and more that happiness is not dependent on health or any other outside prosperity. We are at peace with each other and at peace with God; His dealings with us do not perplex or puzzle us, though we do not pretend to understand them. On the other hand, Martha, with absolutely perfect health, with a husband entirely devoted to her, and with every wish gratified, yet seems always careworn and dissatisfied. Her servants worry her very life out; she misses the homely household duties to which she has been accustomed; and her conscience stumbles at little things and overlooks greater ones. It is very interesting, I think, to study different homes as well as the different characters that form them.

Amelia's girls are quiet, good children to whom their father writes what Mr. Underhill and Martha pronounce "beautiful" letters wherein he always styles himself their "brokenhearted but devoted Father." "Devotion," to my mind, involves self-sacrifice; and I cannot reconcile its use, in this case, with the life of ease he leads while all the care of his children is thrown upon others. But some people, by means of a few such phrases, not only impose upon themselves but upon their friends and pass for persons of great sensibility.

As I have been confined to the house nearly the whole winter, I have had to derive my spiritual support from books; and as Mother gradually recovered, she enjoyed Leighton with me, as I knew she would. Dr. Cabot comes to see us very often, but I do not now find it possible to get the instruction from him I used to do. I see that the Christian life must be individual, as the natural character is, and that I cannot be exactly like Dr. Cabot, or exactly like Mrs. Campbell, or exactly like Mother, though they all three stimulate and are an inspiration to me. But I see, too, that the great points of similarity in Christ's disciples have always been the same. This is the testimony of all the good books, sermons, hymns, and memoirs I read—that God's ways are infinitely perfect; that we are to love Him for what He is and therefore equally as much when He afflicts as when He prospers us; that there is no real happiness but in doing and suffering His will; and that this life is but a scene of probation through which we pass to the real life above.

Oct. 20—

I made a parting visit to Mrs. Campbell today and, as usual, have come away strengthened and refreshed. She said all sorts of kind things to cheer and encourage me and stimulated me to take up the burden of life cheerfully and patiently, just as it comes. She assures me that these fluctuations of feeling will, by degrees, give place to a calmer life, especially if I avoid, so far as I can do it, all unnecessary work, distraction, and hurry. And a few quiet, resting words from her have given me courage to press on toward perfection, no matter how much imperfection I see in myself and others. And now I am waiting for my Father's next gift and the new cares and labors it will bring with it. I am glad it is not left to me to decide my own lot. I am afraid I should never see precisely the right moment for welcoming a new bird into my nest, dearly as I love the rustle of their wings and the sound of their voices when they do come. And surely He knows the right moments who knows all my struggles with a certain sort of poverty, poor health, and domestic care. If I could feel that all the time, as I do at this moment, how happy I should always be!

JANUARY 16, 1847—

This is the tenth anniversary of our wedding day, and it has been a delightful one. If I were called upon to declare what has been the chief element of my happiness, I should say it was not Ernest's love for me or mine for him, or that I am once more the mother of three children, or that my own dear Mother still lives, though I revel in each and all of these. But underneath them all, deeper, stronger than all, lies a peace with God that I can compare to no other joy, which I guard as I would guard hid treasure and which must abide if all things else pass away.

My baby is two months old, and her name is Ethel. The three children together form a beautiful picture that I am never tired of admiring. But they will not give me much time for writing. This little newcomer takes all there is of me. Mother brings me pleasant reports of Miss Clifford, who, under her gentle, wise influence, is becoming an earnest Christian, already rejoicing in the Providence that arrested her where it did and forced her to reflection. Mother says we ought to study God's Providence more than we do, since He has a meaning and a purpose in everything He does. Sometimes I can do this and find it a source of great happiness. Then worldly cares seem mere worldly cares, and I forget that His wise, kind hand is in every one of them.

MARCH—

I know now, and glad I am! The sly little puss is purring at this moment in James's arms; at least I suppose she is, as I have discreetly come up to my room and left them to themselves. So it seems I have had all these worries about Lucy for naught. What made her so fond of James was simply the fact that a friend of his had looked on her with a favorable eye, regarding her as a very proper mother for four or five children who are in need of a shepherd. Yes, Lucy is going to marry a man so much older than herself that on a pinch he might have been her father. She does it from a sense of duty, she says; and to a nature like hers, duty may perhaps suffice and no cry of the heart have to be stifled in its performance. We are all so happy in the happiness of James and Helen that we are not in the mood to criticize Lucy's decision. I have a strange and most absurd envy when I think what a good time they are having at this moment downstairs while I sit here alone, vainly wishing I could see more of Ernest. Just as if my happiness were not a deeper, more blessed one than theirs, which must be purged of much dross before it will prove itself to be like gold. Yes, I suppose I am as happy in my dear, precious husband and children as a wife and mother can be in a fallen world, which must not be a real heaven lest we should love the land we journey through so well as to want to pitch our tents in it forever and cease to look and long for the home whither we are bound.

James will be married almost immediately, I suppose, as he sails for Syria early in April. How much a missionary and his wife must be to each other when, severing themselves from all they ever loved before, they go forth, hand in hand, not merely to be foreigners in heathen lands but to be henceforth strangers in their own should they ever return to it!

Helen says, playfully, that she has not a missionary spirit and is not at all sure that she shall go with James. But I don't think that he feels very anxious on that point!

MARCH—

It does one's heart good to see how happy they are! And it does one's heart good to have one's husband set up an opposition to the goings-on by behaving like a lover himself.

JANUARY 1, 1851—

It is a great while since I wrote that. "God has been just as good as ever"; I want to say that before I say another word. But He has indeed smitten me very sorely.

While we were in the midst of our rejoicings about James and Helen and the bright future that seemed opening before them, he came home one day very ill. Ernest happened to be in and attended to him at once. But the disease was, at the very outset, so violent and raged with such absolute fury that no remedies had any effect. Everything, even now, seems confused in my mind. It seems as if there was a sudden transition from the most brilliant, joyous health to a brief but fearful struggle for life, speedily followed by the awful mystery and stillness of death. Is it possible, I still ask myself, that four short days wrought an event whose consequences must run through endless years? —poor Mother! Poor Helen! When it was all over, I do not know what to say of Mother but that she behaved and quieted herself like a weaned child. Her sweet composure awed me; I dared not give way to my own vehement, terrible sorrow; in the presence of this Christlike patience, all noisy demonstrations seemed profane. I thought no human being was less selfish, more loving than she had been for many years, but the spirit that now took possession of her flowed into her heart and life directly from the great Heart of love, whose depths I had never even begun to sound. There was, therefore, something absolutely divine in her aspect, in the tones of her voice, in the very smile on her face. We could compare its expression to nothing but Stephen, when he, being full of the Holy Ghost, looked up steadfastly to heaven and saw the Glory of God and Jesus standing on the right hand of God. . . .

MARCH 5, 1852—

This is the sixth anniversary of James's death. Thinking it all over after I went to bed last night, his sickness, his death, and the weary months that followed for Mother, I could not get to sleep till long past midnight. Then Una woke, crying with the earache, and I was up till nearly daybreak with her, poor child. I got up jaded and depressed, almost ready to faint under the burden of life and dreading to meet Helen, who is doubly sad on these anniversaries. She came down to breakfast dressed as usual in deep mourning and looking as spiritless as I felt. The prattle of the children relieved the somber silence maintained by the rest of us, each of whom acted depressingly on the others. How things do flash into one's mind! These words suddenly came to mine, as we sat so gloomily at the table God had spread for us and which He had enlivened by the four young faces around it—

> *Why should the children of a King*
> *Go mourning all their days? . . .*

MARCH 30—

A stormy day and the children home from school, and no little frolicking and laughing going on. It must be delightful to feel well and strong while one's children are young; there is so much to do for them. I do it; but no one can tell the effort it costs me. What a contrast there is between their vitality and the languor under which I suffer! When their noise became intolerable, I proposed to read to them; of course they made ten times as much clamor of pleasure and of course they leaned on me, ground their elbows into my lap, and tired me all out. As I sat with this precious little group around me, Ernest opened the door, looked in gravely and without a word, and instantly disappeared. I felt uneasy and asked him this evening why he looked so. Was I indulging the children too much, or what was it? He took me into his arms and said:

"My precious wife, why will you torment yourself with such fancies? My very best heart was yearning over you at that moment, as it did the first time I saw you surrounded by your little class at Sunday school years ago, and I was asking myself why God had given me such a wife and my children such a mother."

Oh, I am glad I have got this written down! I will read it over when the sense of my deficiencies overwhelms me, while I ask God why He has given me such a patient, forbearing husband.

APRIL 1—

This has been a sad day for our church. Our dear Dr. Cabot has gone to his eternal home and left us as sheep without a shepherd.

His death was sudden at the last and found us all unprepared for it. But my tears of sorrow are mingled with tears of joy. His heart had long been in heaven; he was ready to go at a moment's warning; never was a soul so constantly and joyously on the wing as his. Poor Mrs. Cabot! She is left very desolate, for all their children are married and settled at a distance. But she bears this sorrow like one who has long felt herself a pilgrim and a stranger on earth. How strange that we ever forget that we are all such!

APRIL 16—

The desolate pilgrimage was not long. Dear Mrs. Cabot was this day laid away by the side of her beloved husband, and it is delightful to think of them as not divided by death but united by it in a complete and eternal union.

I never saw a husband and wife more tenderly attached to each other, and this is a beautiful close to their long and happy married life. I find it hard not to wish and pray that I may as speedily follow my precious husband, should God call him away first. But it is not for me to choose.

How I shall miss these faithful friends who, from my youth up, have been my stay and my staff in the house of my pilgrimage! Almost all the disappointments and sorrows of my life have had their Christian sympathy, particularly the daily, wasting solicitude concerning my darling Una, for they, too, watched for years over as delicate a flower and saw it fade and die. Only those who have suffered thus can appreciate the heartsoreness through which, no matter how outwardly cheerful I may be, I am always passing. But what then! Have I not ten thousand times made this my prayer that, in the words of Leighton, my will might become "identical with God's will"?

And shall He not take me at my word? Just as I was writing these very words, my canary burst forth with a song so joyous that a song was put also in my mouth. Something seemed to say this captive sings in his cage because it has never known liberty and cannot regret a lost freedom. So the soul of my child, limited by the restrictions of a feeble body, never having known the gladness of exuberant health, may sing songs that will enliven and cheer. Yes, and does sing them! What should we do without her gentle, loving presence, whose frailty calls forth our tenderest affections and whose sweet face makes sunshine in the shadiest places! I am sure that the boys are truly blessed by having a sister always at home to welcome them and that their best manliness is appealed to by her helplessness.

What this child is to me I cannot tell. And yet, if the skillful and kind Gardener should house this delicate plant before frosts come, should I dare to complain?

JUNE 2—

I went to see Mrs. Campbell a few days ago and found, to my great joy, that Helen had just been there and that they had had a long and earnest conversation together. Mrs. Campbell has failed a good deal of late, and it is not probable that we shall have her with us much longer. Her every look and word is precious to me when I think of her as one who is so soon to enter the unseen world, and see our Savior, and be welcomed home by Him. If it is so delightful to be with those who are on the way to heaven, what would it be to have fellowship with one who had come thence and could tell us what it is!

She spoke freely about death and said Ernest had promised to take charge of her funeral and to see that she was buried by the side of her husband.

"You see, my dear," she added with a smile, "though I am expecting to be so soon a saint in heaven, I am a human being still, with human weaknesses. What can it really matter where this weary old body is laid away when I have done with it and gone and left it forever? And yet I am leaving directions about its disposal!"

I said I was glad that she was still human, but that I did not think it a weakness to take thought for the abode in which her soul had dwelt so long. I saw that she was tired and was coming away, but she held me and would not let me go.

"Yes, I am tired," she said, "but what of that? It is only a question of days now, and all my tired feelings will be over. Then I shall be as young and as fresh as ever and shall have strength to praise and to love God as I cannot do now. But before I go, I want once more to tell you how good He is, how blessed it is to suffer with Him, how infinitely happy He has made me in the very hottest heat of the furnace. It will strengthen you in your trials to recall this, my dying testimony. There is no wilderness so dreary but that His love can illuminate it, no desolation so desolate but that He can sweeten it. I know what I am saying. It is no delusion. I believe that the highest, purest happiness is known only to those who have learned Christ in sickrooms, in poverty, in racking suspense and anxiety, amid hardships, and at the open grave."

Yes, the radiant face, worn by sickness and suffering but radiant still, said in language yet more unspeakably impressive, "To learn Christ, this is life!"

I came into the busy and noisy streets as one descending from the mount, and on reaching home found my darling Una very ill in Ernest's arms. She had fallen and injured her head. How I had prayed that God would temper the wind to this shorn lamb, and now she had had such a fall! We watched over her till far into the night, scarcely speaking to each other; but I know by the way in which Ernest held my hand clasped in his that her precious life was in danger. He consented at last to lie down, but Helen stayed with me. What a night it was! God only knows what the human heart can experience in a space of time that men call hours. I went over all the past history of the child, recalling her sweet looks and words and my own secret repining at the delicate health that has cut her off from so many of the pleasures that belong to her age. And the more I thought, the more I clung to her on whom, frail as she is, I was beginning to lean and whose influence in our home I could not think of losing without a shudder.

Alas, my faith seemed for a time to flee, and I could see just what a poor, weak human being is without it. But before daylight crept into my room, light from on high streamed in my heart, and I gave even this, my ewe lamb, away as my freewill offering to God. Could I refuse Him my child because she was the very apple of my eye? Nay then, but let me give to Him not what I value least, but what I prize and delight in most. Could I not endure heartsickness for Him who had given His only Son for me? And just as I got to that sweet consent to suffer, He who had only lifted the rod to try my faith, laid it down. My darling opened her eyes and looked at us intelligently and with her own loving smile. But I dared not snatch her and press her to my heart; for her sake I must be outwardly calm at least.

JUNE 6—

I am at home with my precious Una, all the rest having gone to church. She lies peacefully on the bed, sadly disfigured for the time; but Ernest says he apprehends no danger now, and we are a most happy, a most thankful household. The children have all been greatly moved by the events of the last few days and hover about their sister with great sympathy and tenderness. Where she fell from or how she fell, no one knows; she remembers nothing about it herself, and it will always remain a mystery.

This is the second time that this beloved child has been returned to us after we had given her away to God.

And as the giving cost us tenfold more now than it did when she was a feeble baby, so we receive her now as a fresh gift from our loving Father's hand with tenfold delight. Ah, we have no excuse for not giving ourselves entirely to Him. He has revealed Himself to us in so many sorrows and in so many joys, revealed Himself as He doth not unto the world!

JUNE 13—

This had been a Sunday to be held in long remembrance. We were summoned early this morning to Mrs. Campbell and have seen her joyful release from the fetters that have bound her so long. Her loss to me is irreparable. But I can truly thank God that one more "tired traveler" has had a sweet "welcome home." I can minister no longer to her bodily wants and listen to her councils no more, but she has entered as an inspiration into my life, and through all eternity I shall bless God that He gave me that faithful, praying friend. How little they know who languish in what seem useless sickrooms or amid the restrictions of frail health, what work they do for Christ by the power of saintly living and by even fragmentary prayers.

Before her words fade out of my memory, I want to write down, from hasty notes made at the time, her answer to some of the last questions I asked her on earth. She had always enjoyed intervals of comparative ease, and it was in one of these that I asked her what she conceived to be the characteristics of an advanced state of grace. She replied, "I think that the mature Christian is always, at all times and in all circumstances, what he was in his best moments in the progressive stages of his life. There were seasons, all along his course, when he loved God supremely; when he embraced the cross joyfully and penitently; when he held intimate communion with Christ and loved his neighbor as himself. But he was always in terror lest under the force of temptation all this should give place to deadness and dullness, when he would chafe and rebel in the hour of trial and judge his fellowman with a harsh and bitter judgment and give way to angry, passionate emotions. But these fluctuations cease, after a time, to disturb his peace. Love to Christ becomes the abiding, inmost principle of his life; he loves Him rather for what He is than for what He has done or will do for him individually, and God's honor becomes so dear to him that he feels personally wounded when that is called in question. And the will of God becomes so dear to him that he loves it best when it 'triumphs at his cost.'

"Once he only prayed at times and seasons and idolized good frames and fervent emotions. Now he prays without ceasing and, whether on the mount or down in the depths, depends wholly upon his Savior.

"His old self-confidence has now given place to childlike humility that will not let him take a step alone;

and the sweet peace that is now habitual to him, combined with the sense of his own imperfections, fills him with love for his fellowman. He hears and believes and hopes and endures all things and thinketh no evil. The tones of his voice, the very expression of his countenance become changed, love now controlling where human passions held sway. In short, he is not only a new creature in Jesus Christ, but has the habitual and blessed consciousness that this is so."

These words were spoken deliberately and with reflection.

"You have described my mother just as she was from the moment her only son, the last of six, was taken from her," I said at last. "I never before quite understood how that final sorrow weaned her, so to say, from herself and made her life all love to God and all love to man. But I see it now. Dear Mrs. Campbell, pray for me that I may yet wear her mantle!"

She smiled with a significance that said she had already done so, and then we parted—parted that she might end her pilgrimage and go to her rest—parted that I might pursue mine; I know not how long, nor amid how many cares and sorrows, nor with what weariness and heartsickness—parted to meet again in the presence of Him we love, with those who have come out of great tribulation, whose robes have been made white in the blood of the Lamb, and who are before the throne of God, and serve Him day and night in His temple, to hunger no more, neither thirst any more, for the Lamb which is in the midst of the throne shall lead them into living fountains of waters; and God shall wipe away all tears from their eyes (Revelation 7:14–17).

JUNE 30, 1860—

Everybody wonders to see me once more interested in my long-closed journal and becoming able to see the dear friends from whom I have been, in a measure, cut off. We cannot ask the meaning of this remarkable increase of strength.

I have no wish to choose. But I have come to the last page of my journal and, living or dying, shall write in this volume no more. It closes upon a life of much childishness and great sinfulness, whose record makes me blush with shame; but I no longer need to relieve my heart with seeking sympathy in its unconscious pages, nor do I believe it well to go on analyzing it as I have done. I have had large experience of both joy and sorrow; I have seen the nakedness and the emptiness, and I have seen the beauty and sweetness of life. What I have to say now, let me say to Jesus. What time and strength I used to spend in writing here, let me now spend in prayer for all men, for all sufferers, for all who are out of the way, for all whom I love. And their name is Legion, for I love everybody.

Yes, I love everybody! That crowning joy has come to me at last. Christ is in my soul; He is mine; I am as conscious of it as that my husband and children are mine; and His Spirit flows forth from mine in the calm peace of a river whose banks are green with grass and glad with flowers. If I die, it will be to leave a wearied and worn body and a sinful soul to go joyfully to be with Christ, to weary and to sin no more. If I live, I shall find much blessed work to do for Him. So living or dying, I shall be the Lord's.

But I wish, oh, how earnestly, that whether I go or stay, I could inspire some lives with the joy that is now mine. For many years I have been rich in faith, rich in an unfaltering confidence that I was beloved of my God and

Savior. But something was wanting; I was ever groping for a mysterious grace, the want of which made me often sorrowful in the very midst of my most sacred joy, imperfect when I most longed for perfection. It was the personal love of Christ of which my precious mother so often spoke to me, which she often urged me to seek upon my knees. If I had known then, as I know now, what this priceless treasure could be to a sinful human soul, I would have sold all that I had to buy the field wherein it lay hidden. But not till I was shut up to prayer and to study of God's Word by the loss of earthly joys, sickness destroying the flavor of them all, did I begin to penetrate the mystery that is learned under the cross. And wondrous as it is, how simple is this mystery! To love Christ and to know that I love Him—this is all!

And when I entered upon the sacred yet often homely duties of married life, if this love had been mine, how would that life have been transfigured! The petty faults of my husband under which I chafed would not have moved me; I should have welcomed Martha and her father to my home and made them happy there; I should have had no conflicts with my servants, shown no petulance to my children. For it would not have been I who spoke and acted, but Christ who lived in me.

Alas! I have had less than seven years in which to atone for a sinful, wasted past and to live a new and a Christlike life. If I am to have yet more, thanks be to Him who has given me the victory that life will be Love. Not the love that rests in the contemplation and adoration of its object; but the love that gladdens, sweetens, solaces other lives.